▶ **The Debt Crisis and European Democratic Legitimacy**

DOI: 10.1057/9781137298010

Other Palgrave Pivot titles

Chiara Mio: Towards a Sustainable University: The Ca' Foscari Experience

Jordi Cat: Maxwell, Sutton and the Birth of Color Photography: A Binocular Study

Nevenko Bartulin: Honorary Aryans: National–Racial Identity and Protected Jews in the Independent State of Croatia

Coreen Davis: State Terrorism and Post-transitional Justice in Argentina: An Analysis of Mega Cause I Trial

Deborah Lupton: The Social Worlds of the Unborn

Shelly McKeown: Identity, Segregation and Peace-Building in Northern Ireland: A Social Psychological Perspective

Rita Sakr: 'Anticipating' the 2011 Arab Uprisings: Revolutionary Literatures and Political Geographies

Timothy Jenkins: Of Flying Saucers and Social Scientists: A Re-Reading of When Prophecy Fails and of Cognitive Dissonance

Ben Railton: The Chinese Exclusion Act: What It Can Teach Us about America

Patrick Joseph Ryan: Master-Servant Childhood: A History of the Idea of Childhood in Medieval English Culture

Andrew Dowdle, Scott Limbocker, Song Yang, Karen Sebold, and Patrick A. Stewart: Invisible Hands of Political Parties in Presidential Elections: Party Activists and Political Aggregation from 2004 to 2012

Jean-Paul Gagnon: Evolutionary Basic Democracy: A Critical Overture

Mark Casson and Catherine Casson: The Entrepreneur in History: From Medieval Merchant to Modern Business Leader

Tracy Shilcutt: Infantry Combat Medics in Europe, 1944–45

Asoka Bandarage: Sustainability and Well-Being: The Middle Path to Environment, Society, and the Economy

Panos Mourdoukoutas: Intelligent Investing in Irrational Markets

Jane Wong Yeang Chui: Affirming the Absurd in Harold Pinter

Carol L. Sherman: Reading Olympe de Gouges

Elana Wilson Rowe: Russian Climate Politics: When Science Meets Policy

Joe Atikian: Industrial Shift: The Structure of the New World Economy

Tore Bjørgo: Strategies for Preventing Terrorism

Kevin J. Burke, Brian S. Collier and Maria K. McKenna: College Student Voices on Educational Reform: Challenging and Changing Conversations

Raphael Sassower: Digital Exposure: Postmodern Postcapitalism

Jeffrey Meyers: Remembering Iris Murdoch: Letter and Interviews

Grace Ji-Sun Kim: Colonialism, Han, and the Transformative Spirit

Rodanthi Tzanelli: Olympic Ceremonialism and the Performance of National Character: From London 2012 to Rio 2016

Marvin L Astrada and Félix E. Martín: Russia and Latin America: From Nation-State to Society of States

DOI: 10.1057/9781137298010

palgrave▸pivot

The Debt Crisis and European Democratic Legitimacy

Huw Macartney

Lecturer in International Political Economy, University of Manchester, UK

DOI: 10.1057/9781137298010

First published 2013 by
PALGRAVE MACMILLAN

Palgrave Macmillan in the UK is an imprint of Macmillan Publishers Limited, registered in England, company number 785998, of Houndmills, Basingstoke, Hampshire RG21 6XS.

Palgrave Macmillan in the US is a division of St Martin's Press LLC, 175 Fifth Avenue, New York, NY 10010.

Palgrave Macmillan is the global academic imprint of the above companies and has companies and representatives throughout the world.

Palgrave® and Macmillan® are registered trademarks in the United States, the United Kingdom, Europe and other countries.

ISBN: 978–1–137–29802–7 EPUB
ISBN: 978–1–137–29801–0 PDF
ISBN: 978–1–137–29800–3 Hardback

A catalogue record for this book is available from the British Library.

A catalog record for this book is available from the Library of Congress.

www.palgrave.com/pivot

DOI: 10.1057/9781137298010

Sa aking apat na pinakamamahal: Ang Diyos Ama, Raquel, Asia at Levi. Kayo ay isang maliit na piraso ng kawalang-hanggan sa mundong eto.

DOI: 10.1057/9781137298010

Contents

DOI: 10.1057/9781137298010

DOI: 10.1057/9781137298010

Acknowledgements

I would like to thank Paul Cammack, Stuart Shields, Hugo Radice, Werner Bonefeld, Kees van der Pijl, Gabriel Siles-Brügge, and a series of anonymous reviewers for their incredibly generous and constructive comments on earlier drafts of this manuscript. I also – again – owe a massive thank you to my wife Raquel, and my children Asia and Levi. My world is a better place because of them. And though I would like to blame my son for any errors in the manuscript – due to the cognitive fog that inevitably accompanies a newborn baby – I won't. Finally, though we live in an age in which belief in God is out of fashion, I am firmly convinced that He still holds the key to resolving some of Western society's most profound crises.

DOI: 10.1057/9781137298010

List of Abbreviations

BBTK	Bond van Bedienden, Technici en Kaderleden
ECB	European Central Bank
ECOFIN	Economic and Financial Affairs Council
EESC	European Economic and Social Committee
EERP	European Economic Recovery Plan
EFSF	European Financial Stability Facility
ESM	European Stabilisation Mechanism
EMS	European Monetary System
EMU	Economic and Monetary Union
ETUC	European Trade Union Confederation
FCC	Federal Constitutional Court
GFC	global financial crisis
IMF	International Monetary Fund
LCBG	large and complex banking group
MEP	Member of European Parliament
OECD	Organisation for Economic Co-operation and Development
SGP	Stability and Growth Pact

palgrave▶pivot

www.palgrave.com/pivot

Introduction

Abstract: *This chapter establishes the two competing movements currently gripping Europe: one pressing for the strengthening of the Europeanised mechanisms of economic adjustment, the other resisting it. It argues that these two are internally related, so that the greater the resistance to economic adjustment the more coercive and insulated from this resistance the imposition of market discipline becomes.*

Macartney, Huw. *The Debt Crisis and European Democratic Legitimacy.* Basingstoke: Palgrave Macmillan, 2013. DOI: 10.1057/9781137298010.

Europe is facing both a political crisis of democracy and legitimacy and an economic crisis of debt and competitiveness. There have been a variety of proposed solutions to these crises. Much of the financial press is captivated by questions regarding the 'rescuing powers' of the European Central Bank (ECB), resolution mechanisms and a full banking union, enhancing the competitiveness of peripheral Europe, or fiscal union, and – amongst other things – centralised taxation regimes. The assumption, one supposes, is that if the *economic* problems are resolved the *political* crisis will resolve itself. In contrast, political scientists of various hues have tended to focus on the democratic legitimacy issue, proposing new democratic movements and the re-balancing of European institutions to avoid the opaque 'closed door' policymaking that has dominated the Eurozone crisis thus far. The policies emanating from the corridors of Brussels are arguably less problematic for these writers than the *process* by which decisions have been taken. This book attempts to join these potentially divergent approaches to thinking about the Eurozone debt crisis and the crisis of democratic legitimacy.

The starting point or puzzle that I seek to address can be framed as follows: at face value it appears as though the two movements evidenced in the political and economic crises point in opposing directions. On the one hand, there is clearly a growing social unrest over the Europeanised mechanisms of economic adjustment; on the other, policymakers seem intent on strengthening precisely those institutions that regulate the adjustment process. If this is the case we can perhaps already perceive a common flaw in the two approaches outlined above (if you'll momentarily excuse the oversimplification). For the political crisis will not easily dissipate if the economic problems are resolved, since the very solutions proposed are themselves exacerbating the political crisis; this also means that the substance of the policies does indeed matter, and not simply the processes by which decisions are made.

In explaining this argument, the book suggests that the false and unhelpful separation of the political from the economic here is essentially a case of 'academic' or analytical neglect as opposed to one that exists 'in the real world', as it were. Put differently, there is an extensive body of Political Economy research – with roots in the classical works of Marx, Smith, Ricardo, Weber, and more recently, Keynes, Polanyi and others – that understands the political and the economic as part of a comprehensive whole. More immediately, though perhaps equally elusively, the political problems confronting the Eurozone are also decisively

DOI: 10.1057/9781137298010

economic and vice versa. The point, at this stage, is a more mundane and pragmatic one: namely, that the economists and lawmakers responsible for fixing the Eurozone cannot, and indeed are not, pursuing an entirely economic solution. Their proposals are infused through and through with a theory of the political and, in particular, democratic participation. Likewise, admirable as calls for a re-democratisation of the European polity may be, they arguably buy into the false separation above, assuming that the exigencies of (economic) crisis management have prompted policymakers to *overlook* or temporarily suspend the political domain.

By turning to a critique of the writings of ordo-liberal and neoliberal intellectuals I will instead argue that a particular worldview predominates amongst leading policymakers, giving shape to responses to the Eurozone crisis. The worldview is not a doctrine or creed, it is not entirely internally coherent, indeed it is contested and riddled with contradictions. Neither is it pure ideology though, as if such a thing could exist as a philosophy somehow detached from the real conditions of everyday social existence. These objections aside, it is, however, remarkably ubiquitous amongst the political classes, despite protestations to the contrary. Indeed, the Eurozone crisis has served to polarise views, with the effect that significantly more policymakers subscribe to this view now and are willing to go to great lengths to implement and enforce it. Put as simply as is reasonably possible, it contends that under the ever-increasingly competitive conditions of globalisation, immediate societal wants must be subordinated to sustained capitalist accumulation whenever there is a conflict between the two. Democratic privileges must be suspended in favour of a 'market police' state. The assumption is that, in the long run, economic growth and prosperity will create trickle-down effects to benefit all social groups.

So far we are perhaps on very familiar territory. The important point to note is that this broad *economic* proposition implicitly contains a particular conception of democracy that is highly political in character. Again, simply, it suggests that society does not necessarily perceive its own best economic interest, instead opting for short-term gains over the conditions for profitable accumulation in the long-term. In the following chapter I will unpack this claim more fully and explain the ordo- and neoliberal conceptions of the democracy question. Chapters 2 to 4 then seek to trace the crystallisation of this form of undemocratic statecraft – the worldview in action, if you like – through the different phases of the Eurozone crisis itself.

As should now be clear, the aim of this book is therefore *pragmatic* insofar as I seek to examine the politics of the debt crisis that I see as

DOI: 10.1057/9781137298010

inherently asymmetrical. A re-constitution of social relations in favour of capital is underway, with European societal groups increasingly subjected to the disciplines of the market over ever-greater realms of social existence. In later chapters I propose three big practical conclusions: the first is that the kinds of protest and resistance movement currently emerging will continue to experience significant difficulties since, for the most part, they have sought to make their voice heard through traditional democratic channels at a time when politics and policymaking is making a decisive departure from democratic methods of leadership. Instead, a more coercive and depoliticised – by which I mean insulated from democratic pressures (Burnham, 2001) – statecraft is taking hold.

The second big conclusion though is that, for policymakers too there are limitations. A number of political thinkers – from Gramsci to Habermas – have emphasised the necessity of popular legitimacy as a requisite to sustained capitalist accumulation. To misquote them, they contended that an economic solution – renewed economic growth for example – would prove to be a sticking plaster over a far deeper social crisis at the very heart of capitalist development; the consent or reluctant acquiescence of subordinate social groups would be required to bind them into the capital relation and contain their aspirations. Yet the politics of depoliticisation has limits in this regard, with the result that current strategies risk turning the debt and democracy crises into a crisis of the state itself and one of the existing socio-economic order.

The third big conclusion focuses on the need for resistance groups to overcome the deep counter-position of the national and international, symptomatic of methodological nationalism. At present, the perceived (and real) fragmentation of European society prevents societal groups from recognising their shared interest and acting collectively. I will argue in the conclusion that the current conjuncture awaits a moment of decisive political intervention, and the book seeks to contribute to other analyses informing resistance and protests against the undemocratic management of the global financial and Eurozone debt crises.

Debt and democracy crises

The nature of the analytical puzzle that frames this book can now be stated more fully. On the one hand, Europe is facing a crisis of debt and competitiveness. Confronted with the speculation of international

DOI: 10.1057/9781137298010

financial markets and their functional representatives – credit rating agencies – policymakers within Europe are attempting to cut public deficits and improve competitiveness. International markets have, since late 2009, repeatedly signalled concerns over the long-term sustainability of high public deficits. The stated rationale is that they threaten economic and financial stability. The less widely publicised reality is that they also reflect a weakness of state actors to impose market disciplines on labour and money; hence the connection with competitiveness reforms (Radice, 2011). Competitiveness is, of course, a deliberately all-encompassing term (van Apeldoorn, 2002). Broadly speaking, it captures concerns over the size of the public sector, social spending (on areas such as healthcare and unemployment), and weak relations between wages and productivity. The prima facie conclusion is that policymakers face pressures from international financial markets to re-structure and reduce. The failure or slow response of the political classes had resulted in revised credit ratings for the sovereign debt of not just 'weaker' peripheral economies, but 'stronger' core economies like Spain and France as well.

On the other hand, the global financial crisis and the ensuing Eurozone crisis seem only to have heightened the sense of disconnect between European electorates and the high-level politics of Brussels. Prior to the financial crisis, though electorates were arguably sceptical about further political integration, reflected in the referenda on the European Constitution, the so-called 'democratic deficit' was more of a concern for academics and practitioners. In part, this was because the politics of everyday lived experience – wage and tax policy, unemployment and retirement benefits – were matters for the nation state. Yet the myth that Brussels was somehow detached from such matters vanished with the Eurozone crisis. Bank bailouts and public spending cuts raised angst towards the domestic elites; while the 'austerity doctrine' – manifest *inter alia* in the Fiscal Compact and the European Semester – espoused and increasingly enforced by European political classes has also focused discontent on Brussels. The logic and benefits of integration have been questioned, as has the right for European actors to impose policy decisions.

The result is that domestic and European policymakers alike have struggled, in the first instance, to formulate a coherent policy programme to address the demands of international capital; and in the second instance, to secure the requisite legitimacy for such policies in the eyes of European society. Together these crises of coherence and legitimacy (Habermas, 1973) threaten the very fabric of the European project.

DOI: 10.1057/9781137298010

Re-democratising Europe

Faced with these challenges, a growing number of commentators have proposed, in various forms, a re-democratisation of the European polity. Their starting premise is the idea that democracy and transparency have been 'the biggest victims of the Euro crisis' (Persson, 2012a). Faced with 'necessary economic reforms' policymakers have consistently run up against 'basic democratic principles' (ibid.). As a result, these commentators argue that the powers of national leaders – *inter alia* – to make decisions on taxation and spending have been neutered; 'democratic responsibility in the governing of Europe' has given way to 'oligarchy' (Daley, 2011). The 'preservation of a democratic Europe that is concerned about societal well-being' has come under attack by the 'unilateral imposition' of 'savage' and 'indiscriminate' cuts (Sen, 2012). This equates to the replacement of 'democratic commitments by financial dictates' (ibid.).

At the heart of the matter is the claim that 'a dangerous asymmetry has developed because to date the European Union has been sustained and monopolised only by political elites' (Habermas, 2011a); and yet with the economic crisis, European citizens have begun to realise 'how deeply the decisions of the European Union pervade their everyday lives', and hence aspire to make use of their 'democratic rights' (ibid.). That is to say that at precisely the time when policymaking has become increasingly opaque and undemocratic, citizens are attempting to engage in more sustained and substantive ways with the European policy process. Though the demands are arguably for 'less' rather than 'more' Europe, or certainly a Europe of a different character.

Noting this tension, other commentators have therefore been more prescriptive in their analysis. Vivien Schmidt (2012), for example, has argued for a re-democratisation of the European Union. The problem, it appears, is that the balance of power between European institutions has become further unsettled through the course of the crisis: decision-making processes have increasingly combined 'excessive intergovernmentalism with technocracy'; the European Council has monopolised decision-making at the expense of the European Parliament (EP); and the European Commission has lost its role as initiator, being demoted to that of a mere secretariat (Schmidt, 2012). The exigencies of crisis management have prompted policymakers to (momentarily?) sidestep time-consuming democratic politics; exacerbating the sense of detachment between high-level processes and the European electorate at precisely

DOI: 10.1057/9781137298010

the time when European policies are perceived to have an ever-greater impact on everyday social existence. Thus 'what the Eurozone needs now is not only new policies and better leadership in the Council but also a more involved European Parliament and a more political Commission President, legitimated via parliamentary election' (ibid.).

Elsewhere, Brendan Simms (2012) has argued for a 'closer and more perfect union', by which he means the 'immediate creation of a fiscal and military union of the continent', complete with a Union parliament, the federalising of state debt, and a single European army. This would be achieved through the formation of a pan-European 'Party of the Democratic Union', expressing the democratic will of the citizens and involving the overthrow of national forms of sovereignty (ibid.: 62). The problem, in his view, is that the renewed shift towards 'economic government' will ultimately fail without the accompanying 'direct democratic participation of the citizens of Europe' (ibid.: 60). As he points out, since they are the ones being forced to advance large sums of money and bear the brunt of structural reforms they must 'buy-in' to the new settlement for it to achieve credibility (ibid.: 49).

For both Schmidt and Simms then, the question of legitimacy is decisive. Whilst acknowledging the struggles policymakers face in formulating a coherent strategy to manage the 'debt crisis', both writers contend that the sheer extent of the political and economic costs will prove to be unbearable, unless legitimacy can be secured. Implicitly they assume, however, that *consent* is the (only) means by which to secure this legitimacy. Indeed, for them, legitimacy is the requirement and democracy the answer. In what follows I will briefly sketch out the key argument of this book which can now be stated as follows: that there are strong reasons to believe that – despite the paradox that this entails – the response of European state managers deliberately seeks to implement institutional and legal changes to insulate policymaking from democratic demands. This is a process called depoliticisation.

I suggest that, from the perspective of the ruling classes, democracy is part of the set of problems that caused the crisis; it cannot therefore simultaneously be part of the solution. This seems to echo the concerns of Commission President Jose Manuel Barroso, who stated that: 'Governments are not always right. If governments were always right we would not have the situation that we have today. Decisions taken by the most democratic institutions in the world are very often wrong' (Barroso, 2010a). To substantiate this claim I draw on a reading of the ordo-liberal – or what has been called German neo-liberal (Sally, 1996) – and (Anglo-American) neoliberal intellectual traditions.

In the following chapter I argue that through the crises of accumulation since the 1950s, a growing disquiet over the 'economic consequences of democracy' began to surface (Brittan, 1976). Framed by the conclusions of ordo- and neoliberal writers, I argue that the project of European integration was not simply elite-driven (Moss, 2000), but fundamentally subordinated social concerns to market imperatives, and established an increasingly coercive and yet depoliticised policy apparatus. Depoliticisation was thus an attempt to place at one remove the political character of decision-making. It allowed state managers to retain a degree of control over economic and social processes whilst shielding them from criticism over unpopular policies. The aim was to change market expectations about the effectiveness and credibility of policymaking (Burnham, 2001). At the time of onset of the global financial crisis (GFC) in 2007 the European arm of this project was, however, incomplete. The GFC – and subsequent debt crisis – therefore provided an opening for political agency.

The main arguments of the book then draw primarily upon a close reading of EU-level documents. Chapter 2 examines the first phase of the crisis, where state managers sought to use the initial financial collapse to promote *neoliberal* structural reform, and to overcome obstacles and opposition.[1] Chapter 3 focuses on the challenge that the emergent debt crisis (late in 2009) posed to the reform process, arguing that the shift towards further depoliticisation was the main political response. Chapter 4, however, addresses some of the limits to depoliticisation as a coherent policy strategy. It highlights the rise of progressively more politicised forms of resistance, arguing that this politicisation itself emanated from the *selective intervention* – to restore capitalist accumulation whilst cutting social spending – of state managers (Burnham, 2011). The conclusion finally questions whether depoliticisation will indeed manage to provide the requisite legitimacy and looks at the potential openings available to resist movements.

In particular, the conclusion I draw from the writings of Rosa Luxemburg and Jürgen Habermas is that there are limits to depoliticisation as a governing strategy. Capitalist development propagates an increasing interventionism on the part of the state. Yet the form and means of this interventionism over time reveals the fundamental subordination of democratic freedoms to capitalist imperatives (Luxemburg, 1898[1973], p.27). Moreover, this interventionism involves the increasing

DOI: 10.1057/9781137298010

reach of the state into previously taken-for-granted areas of life; a process which simultaneously politicises ever more aspects of social existence (Habermas, 1973, p.647). Put differently, interventionism also paradoxically politicises the social groups it disadvantages in a way that can be seen (empirically speaking) through the rise of resistance movements during the debt crisis.

The result is that the increasing interventionism of the state necessitates increasing legitimation if it is to prove sustainable. Yet this legitimation cannot be entirely ad hoc, it must be related and relatable to the extant socio-cultural system that is slower to change and prone to 'stickiness' (Habermas, 1973, p.657). Put differently, attempts to depoliticise policymaking are running up against a European society that has yet to decisively reject the concessions and compromises of the social democratic state. Again, further attempts to entirely protect policymaking from loci of social conflict are therefore also likely to be challenged by increasingly politicised resistance movements.

Finally, I briefly consider the writings on methodological nationalism to show how the deep counter-position of the national with the international continues to frame elite responses and, in turn, hinder resistance movements (Radice, 2000, p.12). In sum, I offer the following conclusions. Firstly, the tension between capitalism and democracy at the heart of the institutions of government/governance suggests that resistance directed through non-traditional, non-democratic channels may be more effective in the long run. Secondly, that depoliticisation fuels a series of counter-movements that it will find difficult to overcome. Thirdly, that a more substantive transnationalisation of resistance movements is necessary to overcome the deep fragmentation of European societal groups.

Note

1   As I explain in the following chapter, I use the term *neoliberal* to encompass both German ordo- and Anglo-American neoliberal traditions. Put simply, rhetorical differences between the two traditions mask the fundamental reconfiguring of social relations in favour of capital that has characterised processes of *neoliberalisation*.

DOI: 10.1057/9781137298010

1

The Free Market and Democracy

Abstract: *This chapter begins with a critical analysis of the ordo-liberal and neoliberal intellectual traditions. It shows how this neoliberal mindworld gave shape to early efforts at economic and monetary integration. It also explains that the neoliberal project – to re-structure European social relations in favour of capital and insulate policymaking from democratic pressures – was incomplete at the time of the global financial crisis in 2007.*

Macartney, Huw. *The Debt Crisis and European Democratic Legitimacy.* Basingstoke: Palgrave Macmillan, 2013. DOI: 10.1057/9781137298010.

DOI: 10.1057/9781137298010

As the previous chapter explained, Europe is facing both a political crisis of democracy and legitimacy and an economic crisis of debt and competitiveness. Pithily, it suggested that as segments of an increasingly politicised European society press for less Europe so the Europeanised mechanisms of economic adjustment are tightened and strengthened. Policymakers have struggled, in the first instance, to construct a coherent strategy; yet the determinant factor, it has been suggested, is the requisite legitimacy in the eyes of European society. This chapter aims to explain – in conceptual terms – why this legitimacy will not centre on greater democratic participation, but rather on the success or failure of *depoliticisation* as a governing strategy. Subsequent chapters then trace the struggle between this attempted further depoliticisation in EU politics and the re-politicisation of European society, before the conclusion addresses the limits of depoliticisation through a look at Habermas and Luxemburg.

Debt and democracy crises

To begin, let us return to the notion of democracy and debt crises. The dominant narrative for explaining the debt crisis emphasises the impact that the global financial crisis (GFC) had on sovereign debt. The connections between rapidly escalating deficits post-2007 and (longer term) issues of structural reform and competitiveness are therefore less prominent. Indeed, this would seem sensible given that debt levels (as a percentage of GDP) rose rapidly from 2008 and bond yields only began to widen from late 2009 onwards. Greek debt, for example, remained relatively stable at 97–107 per cent of GDP until the end of 2007 and Euro area debt remained below 70 per cent of GDP until late 2008 (ECB, 2012).

Yet no astute observer could also fail to recognise the contradictions at the heart of the Eurozone, specifically those that contrasted with expectations of productivity convergence within the single currency area (see Hall, 2013 for an excellent critique of the economic perspectives shaping monetary union). These contradictions were such that, in the lead up to the global financial crisis there were clear signs of a two-tiered Europe, or of export-led growth driven primarily by the core and supplemented, at least in part, by markets in the periphery. For example, whilst Germany, France, Holland and Finland maintained an average fiscal deficit of only 1 per cent for the period 2004–2006, Italy, Spain, Greece and Portugal

DOI: 10.1057/9781137298010

had a mean deficit of 4.4 per cent for the same period. Moreover, these same periphery countries witnessed a significant decline in competitive position vis-à-vis the rest of the Euro area (Commission, 2008a, p.58). This, of course, reflected a variety of factors, not least (those enigmatically captured under the umbrella of) the historical, cultural, institutional and economic starting points of entry to the Economic and Monetary Union, which gave rise to structural imbalances within the zone. The contradictions, however, also reflected a fundamental tension between the elite-driven aspirations that underpinned the integration project, and residual democratic settlements at the domestic level. Indeed, the literature on the so-called 'democratic deficit' in the European Union indicates as much.

This literature is vast. A 'standard version' was however proposed by Follesdal and Hix (2006). It focused on the following themes. First, at the European level, the European Parliament held relatively weak legislative powers vis-à-vis the executive powers of the Council and Commission (Andersen and Burns, 1996; Raunio, 1999). At the national level in all EU member states, the traditional model of democratic politics centres around executive government accountable to the electorate through an elected parliament. In principle, though parliaments have relatively few formal powers of amendment the structure of politics at least allows for the scrutiny of ministers.

This strand of the literature then argues that national ministers operating in the European Union are far more independent of this (national) parliamentary scrutiny. Accordingly, European integration 'has meant a decrease in the power of national parliaments and an increase in the power of executives' (Follesdal and Hix, 2006, p.535, Coultrap, 1999, p.107). Put differently, democracy – referred to as a method by which society exercises influence on the executive apparatus – would seem to have broken down. A 'democratic deficit' indicates that the intended flow of influence from people to government is inadequate in the European context.

Second, the European electorate has little or no input into the selection of parties and personalities at the European level or the direction of the EU policy agenda, in spite of the growing power of the European parliament (Marks et al., 2002). Instead, national elections are fought on domestic issues with parties deliberately avoiding 'European' questions wherever possible. Then European elections themselves are treated as 'second-order national contests' (Reif and Schmitt, 1980), with parties and the media construing them as mid-term national elections. The result is that EU citizens have, at best, an indirect influence over the political agenda of Europe's elected officials.

Third, is the argument that both institutionally and psychologically the EU remains too 'distant' from voters. Not only is electoral control over the Council and Commission ineffectual as discussed above, the EU itself is also markedly different from national systems, making it difficult to comprehend for EU citizens. Connected to this, of course, are relatively opaque and unusual institutions like the Commission, neither government nor bureaucracy and elected through an obscure procedure; and the Council, which is part legislature, part executive and makes its most important decisions in secret.

The fourth theme, however, is particularly illuminating for the argument presented here. Here there is evidence of 'policy drift' whereby 'the EU adopts policies that are not supported by a majority of citizens in many or even most Member States' (Follesdal and Hix, 2006, p.537). To suggest that policy decisions are taken without the participation of the citizens would only be the sum of the previously mentioned weaknesses. Yet this claim goes further still. In particular, governments are able to pursue policies at the European level which are constrained by social democratic-type compromises at the national level, meaning that the pursuit of neoliberal regional regulation and monetarist policy tend to be to the right of the domestic policy status quo. Indeed, one might add to this collection the work of Fritz Scharpf, who also sought to emphasise how the institutions of the European Union asymmetrically structure interest representation and policy negotiation; here policymaking is dominated by non-political actors and negative, rather than positive, integration (Scharpf, 2010, pp. 213–214). In his view the more socially inclusive market economies of continental Europe thus struggle to reproduce their institutions and policies at the European level.

In essence, this begins to reveal the fundamental tension between the elite-driven European project and residual democratic settlements at the domestic level. The counter-argument proposed by – *inter alia* – Giandomenico Majone is that such tensions are inevitable given the desire to achieve Pareto-efficient outcomes at the European level (Majone, 1998, p.6). Regional *economic* integration is in the best interests of European citizens, while political authority is best maintained at a national level (ibid., p.7). Put differently, European elites have a better view of what constitutes the European economic interest – that

DOI: 10.1057/9781137298010

will simultaneously benefit European society in the long-run – than do segments of the European electorate who would, almost inevitably, opt for their own short-term, individualistic self-interest. As we shall see below, this counter-argument resonates with the writings of both ordo- and neoliberal intellectuals and the architects of European integration, though with important qualifiers. For now, suffice it to note that there was evidence – even prior to the onset of the Eurozone debt crisis – of resistance from domestic social groups to the policies consistent with the elite vision of European (economic and monetary) integration.

Ordo- and neo-liberals on democracy and the free market

To explain this more fully I now turn to a reading of the ordo- and neoliberal traditions on the question of the free market and democracy. In essence, the challenge posed by democratic demands is a familiar one. This is because there has long been – across the advanced economies – a growing disquiet over the 'economic consequences of democracy' (Brittan, 1976). Put simply, 'excessive expectations' on the part of electorates were fuelled by the 'democratic aspects of the system', whereby social demands were seen to have overstretched the welfare state (ibid., p.97). The post-war settlement had allowed for full employment and welfare because of the booming economy, and thus signalled a 'conscious acceptance on the part of national governments of [the demands of] mass society and mass democracy' (Bonefeld, 2002, p.122). Yet the end of the post-war boom revealed the merely formal involvement of the dependent masses, integrated into the political economy of capital only to contain their political aspirations. Thus the post-war welfare state was embedded in a European structure of market competition (Moss, 2000).

As these crises of accumulation emerged two intellectual traditions were pivotal to attempts to understand the causes. One was closely associated with the work of Milton Friedman, Friedrich Hayek and the Mont Pelerin Society, and is commonly characterised as (Anglo-Saxon) neoliberalism. The other which emerged from the Freiburg School was closely associated with the work of Walter Eucken, Franz Böhm, Alexander Rüstow, Wilhelm Röpke and Alfred Müller-Armack and was known as ordo-liberalism.

DOI: 10.1057/9781137298010

For Hayek and Friedman, the aim was to free the economy from political interference, depoliticising economic relations such that the market could self-regulate (Hayek, 1949). Thus 'active public economic policy [was, in their view] either redundant or, more likely, perverse' (Best, 2005, p.92). Not only governmental intrusion but strong trade unions too were to be avoided. Instead, the relationship between the money supply and labour productivity would be strengthened through the deregulation and flexibilisation of the labour market, accompanied by the shift from welfare to workfare. Thus, in response to what they perceived as the inflationary consequences of Keynesianism, Hayek in particular advocated the depoliticisation of economic policymaking from political – that is *discretionary* – intervention in the short-term interests of the working classes.

For Müller-Armack and the ordo-liberals, regulative laws and institutions were needed in order – not to interfere with the market process but –to sustain it (Müller-Armack, 1947, p.95). This meant that the ordo-liberals favoured a strong state – not of the *dirigiste* type but – as the pre-condition for the free market, since the mass of society lacked the 'moral fabric' to absorb economic adjustments, preferring short-term policy responses that favoured employment and welfare (Röpke, 2009, p.52; 1942, pp.246–247). An 'extra-democratic' body would thereby govern in the name of technical efficiency and expertise, without interference from mass demands. Given that the true interest of the worker lay in continued accumulation, social security and employment, the threat that democracy posed to liberalism was not insignificant (Müller-Armack, 1979, pp.146–147). The movement of the free-price mechanism, the ordo-liberals concluded, had the capacity to regulate between multifarious individual preferences, except that its participants 'rebel against that movement' (Böhm, 1937, p.11; Bonefeld, 2012, p.5). This could occur equally through entrepreneurs opposing the pressures of competitive adjustment as it could through the self-destructive demands for welfare on the part of workers. Thus, for the ordo-liberals the solution was the depoliticisation of society to tackle the subordination of the political to mass democratic demands.

The point is that both ordo- and neoliberal traditions had concerns about the distortive potential of democracy. Indeed, and to (mis)quote Simon Clarke, 'there is no doubt that the rise of [German and Anglo-American traditions are] the ideological expression of fundamental changes in the form of the state, that have reflected, and reinforced, the

DOI: 10.1057/9781137298010

massive political defeat of the working class' (Clarke, 1988, p.223). For this reason, and because both traditions were fundamental to the construction of economic and monetary union and particularly the German vision of how to resolve the Eurozone crisis, I will henceforth predominantly refer to *neoliberalism*. For despite protestations to the contrary, rhetorical differences between the two mystify the fundamental re-structuring of class relations and political intervention, in favour of capital, that has characterised variegated processes of *neoliberalisation* (Macartney 2010).[1] In what follows, I address the former component – the design of European integration – whilst the latter – attempts to resolve the Eurozone crisis – frames the analysis of later chapters.

It was thus Hayek whose vision of a federal interstate system in Europe was remarkably prescient. He contended that a supranational political architecture would foster competitiveness, and the depoliticisation of economic relations, whilst – of course – allowing for the free movement of capital, labour and goods (Hayek, 1939, pp.255–268). Since national governments, committed as they claim to be to the objective of price stability, necessarily retain a degree of discretion that, in his view, makes them liable to exploit it to gain electoral popularity by granting concessions to the dependent masses. Giving monetary policy to an institution that is not subject to political influence would thus enhance its credibility (Padoa-Schioppa, 1994, p.188). Put differently, and here there was a certain confluence with the work of – in particular – Müller-Armack, a domestic politics of austerity could be anchored in a supranational regime (Müller-Armack, 1979). Thus supranationalism, and especially the primacy of the rule of law, and an independent central bank were 'endorsed as a way of keeping the masses *away* from the centre of decision making' (*emphasis added* Bonefeld, 2002, p.130).

The structure of integration

The first attempt, the so-called 'snake in the tunnel' – a European exchange rate system where currencies fluctuated within an agreed margin against the dollar, failed; countries were repeatedly forced to suspend membership because of speculative pressures. Importantly though, these speculative pressures were themselves the product of working class resistance to the imposition of tougher working conditions. Then, in the late 1970s, the European Exchange Rate Mechanism – part of the European

DOI: 10.1057/9781137298010

Monetary System (EMS) – was introduced to combat currency fluctuations and address underlying domestic challenges. It too struggled.

The 1980s witnessed a much more severe approach as brief experiments with fiscal and monetary expansionism – particularly under Mitterrand in France – were ill-fated and led to a stricter EMS and tighter monetary policy. The disciplinary effect on wage demands and working conditions was undeniable, with wage increases and higher productivity moderated by the threat of unemployment. Disinflation would be achieved by shifting the burden of adjustment onto labour. The logic was clear: fiscal, social, and labour-market policies were now subordinated to the holy grail of price stability through labour-market deregulation and flexibilisation (Bieler, 2006, p.13; van Apeldoorn, 2002).

In turn, the shift from welfare to workfare took hold: poverty would be addressed by equipping individuals for employment. Though a plausible way to reduce the apparently 'overstretched' state, the cruel irony was that the overall size of the workforce was maximised so individuals would be forced to compete for employment, with competition itself made as intense as possible (Cammack, 2007, p.16). For domestic state managers European integration provided a means of externalising the imperative for austerity, thereby eroding working class opposition, and anchoring currency stability in a supranational framework.

Hence Europe was necessarily an elite-driven project (Anderson, 1997, p.62). For centre-left parties, integration was a 'way of defending the market economy against Communism while retaining a humanitarian internationalist identity' (Moss, 2000, p.251). Yet according to Moss, this masked the reality that the single market and monetary union reflected tightened capitalist domination (ibid., p.252). For centre-right parties this reality was more apparent, as Europe provided the means to impose market disciplines on industry, to increase labour productivity and competitiveness. As De Gaulle (1971, p.143) surmised, 'international competition ... offered a lever to stimulate our business sector' that diverted the focus away from French policymakers. Whilst for capitalists in industry, finance and agriculture, the single market operating under a tight monetary policy was a means to undermine national social regulations and promote wage restraint (Bieler, 2006, pp.12–13). Indeed, 'why should a "domestic" bourgeoisie not wish that "its" working class is made to work harder and for declining wages, and to achieve this in a way which makes it appear as if the bourgeoisie is not responsible for the burden placed on labour?' (Bonefeld, 1998, p.58).

DOI: 10.1057/9781137298010

Certainly, the cumulative effects of liberalisation and denationalisation that took hold were in many ways unforeseen by the founders of integration (Moss, 2000, p.252). Unpredicted cyclical changes, both up and down, accompanied by increased worker mobilisation and welfare spending that compounded the profitability squeeze and the crisis of the Keynesian interventionist state, served to polarise social forces and resulted in renewed liberalisation and integration (Bieler, 2006).

Nonetheless, the key principles of integration reflected a clear ordoliberal bias: its 'use of competitive markets with low external tariffs and sound money backed by an independent bank dedicated to price stability to counter the inflationary tendencies of over-spending governments and demanding workers and unions' (Moss, 2000, p.258).

As the 1990s unfolded, it became all the more apparent that the currency union was informed by the attempt to depoliticise policymaking. Michael Emerson explained that 'a stable and credible monetary regime requires an independent central bank with the statutory mandate to guarantee price stability ... [since] in democratic societies elected officials are in general free to determine economic policy at their discretion' making it 'very difficult for *political* bodies to acquire enough credibility' (Emerson,1992, pp.87, 97, emphasis added). Moreover, for Tommaso Padoa-Schioppa, this collective decision-making mechanism thereby increasingly replaced national hegemony over monetary policy – and hence national centres as focal points of social and political struggle – with community centralised institutions (1994). The Maastricht Treaty (1992) thus further endorsed the principles of price stability and competitive markets, while the European Central Bank was founded with extra precautions to ensure that it was not influenced by national political leaders. Without a common European government – and accompanying economic priorities – Economic and Monetary Union (EMU) established the stability and convergence criteria in an attempt to constrain national budgetary deficits and debt.

EMU institutionally reinforced the separation of political from economic considerations, on the premise that the management of the European economy was too sensitive and significant an issue to be disrupted by political expediency; it insulated 'key economic agents, especially [the European] Central Bank, from interference by elected politicians' (Gill, 1995, p.168; see also Shields, 2007). This was because the distributive implications of the separation between monetary policy and price stability – under the auspices of EU-level institutions and the

DOI: 10.1057/9781137298010

European Central Bank – and welfare and labour market policy – in the hands of member state governments – had, as indicated above, long been a concern for core Franco-German political classes (Gros and Thygensen, 1992, p.35).[2] The rise in supranational economic policymaking was intended to remove from national elites both the freedom of and responsibility for a 'distasteful' politics of austerity; such initiatives were now *imposed* from above by European-level institutions, empowering the national government to argue their own impotency in the face of mounting pressure from their electorate.

To summarise, the defining feature of European integration is its attempt to construct a free-market mechanism that is progressively more insulated from working class aspirations. To quote Bonefeld, it sought to 'inscribe the neo-liberal policy of market freedom associated with Hayek through the creation of constitutional devices associated with [German] ordo-liberalism' (Bonefeld, 1998, pp.67; 2005, p.93). The means to achieve this is via the commitment to and construction of Europeanised mechanisms of economic adjustment, under the rubric of sound money and rules-based governance (Young, 2012). The point was that these depoliticised mechanisms effectively removed the *impetus* for adjustment from domestic bourgeoisies, whilst placing the *burden* of adjustment firmly on domestic working classes.

An incomplete project

In reality however, the European project was only partially complete as the global financial crisis began to unfold in 2007. The very fact that the neoliberal Lisbon agenda had entered a second phase in 2005 was evidence, for example, of the growing awareness that the challenges of structural reform and competitiveness had not been met. Beginning with the Kok Report (2004, p.7) the EU had acknowledged that 'the European Union and its Members States have clearly themselves contributed to slow progress by failing to act on much of the Lisbon strategy with sufficient urgency'. The problem was one of implementation, with the Kok Report noting that 'the Lisbon strategy is even more urgent today as the growth gap with North America and Asia has widened, while Europe must meet the combined challenges of low population growth and ageing. Time is running out and there can be no room for complacency. Better implementation is needed to make up for lost time' (ibid.).

DOI: 10.1057/9781137298010

As a result national reform programmes were introduced, whereby plans to address poor productivity, rigid product and labour markets, bureaucratic barriers to public and private investment and innovation, and budgetary discipline were shaped at the national level and subsequently submitted to the Commission for review. Significantly however, by January 2006, as the Commission formulated its first Annual Progress Report on Growth and Jobs, progress remained limited (Commission, 2006a, pp.4–5). From the perspective of European state managers it was 'time to move up a gear' (Council, 2006).

Moreover, EU institutions were not alone in their concerns over remaining resistance to neoliberal structural reforms and the apparent weakness of member state governments in addressing these 'productivity gaps'. In its 2006 report on *Economic Policy Reforms: Going for Growth*, the OECD noted that the EU was lagging approximately 30 per cent behind US GDP per capita. It flagged restrictive entry controls and competition-restraining regulation, including the extent of public ownership in certain EU countries, as important factors. It also highlighted that

> Given their relatively low labour utilisation, corrective policy priorities in this area were concentrated on continental European countries. In many of these countries, labour force participation rates are relatively low, especially among older workers; levels of unemployment are relatively high; and annual working hours are shorter than in other OECD areas. Reforms to reduce disincentives to work were considered to be less pressing outside continental Europe.

As a result, reform of unemployment benefits, work incentives, and the reduction of labour costs in Germany, Belgium, and France were viewed favourably; whilst the lack of such reform of benefits systems in Greece, Luxembourg, the Slovak Republic and Spain was criticised (OECD 2006, pp.11–17).

Similarly, in its article IV comments (2006) the IMF pointed to the need for further fiscal consolidation (UK, France) and reform of overly generous welfare states and labour-market rigidities (France, Germany) (IMF, 2006). Meanwhile the prognosis for peripheral countries was far more damning: in Portugal, rapidly rising labour costs, the collapse of investment, the doubling of unemployment, and rising fiscal deficits were noted (ibid., pp.3–4); in Ireland, the fact that growth was heavily reliant on the construction sector whilst competitiveness had eroded raised concerns (ibid., p.3); and in Spain, despite increases in output growth and employment creation, the fact that the current account deficit had risen

DOI: 10.1057/9781137298010

to 7.5 percentage points of GDP, and the need for 'fostering productivity [through] an early focus on deregulating and opening sheltered sectors to competition', were also flagged (ibid.).

In particular, European integration had paradoxically weakened the pressures for neoliberal (pro-competitive) re-structuring for certain countries, thereby exacerbating the trend of a two-tiered Europe. In effect, Euro entry had led countries like Italy, Spain, Greece and Portugal to accumulate high levels of private and/or public debt and run large current account deficits (Darvas et al., 2011, p.2). These same 'cohesion countries'[3] (Greece, Spain, Ireland, and Portugal in particular), precisely because of the adoption of the Euro, which prompted a downward convergence in interest rates and risk premia had gained increased access to external bank-lending since the mid-1990s. This, coupled *inter alia* with above-average inflation rates (leading to lower real interest rates), demographic changes, and reforms within mortgage markets themselves, had further eased credit conditions (Commission, 2006a, p.28). This meant that their relatively strong performance on paper had been fuelled by investment booms, spurred by capital inflows attracted by comparatively high rates of return, with the single currency and the integration of financial markets acting as a catalyst (Commission, 2008a, p.21). The point, for our purposes here, is that the imperatives of austerity and structural reform – that were central to economic and monetary integration – were diluted by cheap credit and housing equity.

By 2005 the Commission therefore concluded that 'a rigorous prioritisation' and the 'firm support of the European Council and European Parliament' would be required, as well as 'mobilising support for change' so that 'everyone with a stake in Lisbon's success and at every level must be involved in delivering these reforms' (Commission, 2005, p.5). By 2006 the Commission was even more emphatic in its pronunciation that 'at its origin [is] a recognition that success depends on a comprehensive approach, bringing the maximum of levers to bear and touching every corner of every Member State in Europe' (2006a). Yet this approach proved difficult, as the challenges were deep-seated, and conflicting priorities at the national level distracted it from the goal, with slow progress the result (Commission, 2006b). In effect, a crisis of monumental proportions would at least provide the pre-conditions for state managers; forcing the recalcitrant to 'toe the line' and providing the ideal rationalisation for the re-structuring of wage accords, public spending, and social relations more generally in line with European competitiveness.

DOI: 10.1057/9781137298010

Summary

This chapter began with the apparent puzzle that Europe is being gripped by two opposing movements: one pointing towards the strengthening of the supranational mechanisms of economic adjustment and the other resisting precisely this political drive. By drawing on an analysis of the ordo- and neoliberal intellectual traditions it has sought to develop the claim that, from the conditions of sustained crises of accumulation in Europe since the 1950s, a neoliberal political project emerged that sought to establish a free market whilst insulating policymaking from democratic demands. The resistance that it faced arose from democratic settlements and vestiges of the welfare state that European working classes had refused to decisively abandon. The scene is now set for the main focus of this book: an analysis of the three phases of the debt and democracy crises that Europe is experiencing.

Notes

1   Indeed, as Brenner and Theodore – amongst others – have argued, the very conception of Anglo-American neoliberalism as reflective of a laissez-faire economic doctrine is misleading, since though it operates under the rubric of 'free markets liberated from state interference', in practice it entails 'a dramatic intensification of coercive, disciplinary forms of state intervention to impose market rule upon all aspects of social life' (Brenner and Theodore, 2002, p.5).

2   Gros and Thygensen had noted, for example, the concerns of German Chancellor Schmidt over compromises between the Italian ruling class and the communist party (Gros and Thygensen, 1992, p.35).

3   That is, countries that qualified for structural support from EU funds so as to speed up their convergence to EU per-capita income levels.

DOI: 10.1057/9781137298010

2
From Re-structuring to Debt Crisis

Abstract: *This chapter charts the first phase of the global financial crisis as it unfolded in Europe. It focuses on the initial crisis responses of the political classes as they sought to save the banking system, implement stimulus measures, and then capture the crisis moment to renew neoliberal structural reform.*

Macartney, Huw. *The Debt Crisis and European Democratic Legitimacy.* Basingstoke: Palgrave Macmillan, 2013.
DOI: 10.1057/9781137298010.

The previous chapter presented the claim that European integration – as an elite-led project – sought to inscribe the neoliberal policy of market freedom within the framework of strong yet depoliticised constitutional mechanisms. As Moss argues, 'in geopolitical ideological terms it represented the triumph of German ordo-liberalism, a market philosophy that recognised the need for [embedding the free market mechanism within] regulat[ive] laws and institutions' (Moss, 2000, p.252). At its core, the interaction between the ordo- and neoliberal (henceforth simply neoliberal) visions, unforeseen events, and the unintended yet path-dependent consequences of institutional decisions and policies gave rise to a system that privileged sound money and wage restraint in the interests of capital.

I also argued that this project had, however, struggled in the face of the 'stickiness' of existing (dysfunctional) institutions at domestic and European levels, with domestic working classes reluctant to concede their social concessions. This chapter seeks to argue that, as the global financial crisis (GFC) began to unfold, domestic and European state managers quickly sought to channel the crisis hysteria into renewed (neoliberal) structural reform efforts, hoping to overcome this reluctance (Jessop, 2012). The goal was to use the crisis event to rationalise deep reforms that had previously encountered opposition. This, I argue, constituted the first phase of the crisis.

The banking crisis

One might assume, from the argument of the previous chapter, that the evidence of a two-tiered Europe and the concerns of international institutions would have given the EU sufficient forewarning of the impending catastrophe. We know, however, that this was not the case. Indeed, from the European Central Bank's perspective, as Europe entered 2007 the message was rather optimistic. It was particularly keen to emphasise that its role in maintaining price stability and anchoring inflation expectations was again proving successful, with inflation in the Euro area falling to 2.1 per cent. Meanwhile, GDP output had continued to increase at 2.6 per cent, mainly driven through domestic demand and export-led growth, whilst the fiscal deficit ratio for the Euro area declined to 0.8 per cent and unemployment also fell to 7.4 per cent; a level not seen for over 25 years (ECB, 2007, pp.10–12).

EU institutions were therefore largely unprepared for the crisis that was about to unfold, and this was also because the crisis – at least initially – manifested itself as a banking crisis. There were early concerns by the summer of 2007, related to volatile energy prices and heightened uncertainty, and though output had remained resilient and flows of credit appeared unaffected a 'very vigorous' rise in the underlying rate of money and credit expansion throughout 2007 prompted 'precautionary measures' on the part of the ECB Governing Council. In March and June 2007 the Council raised the key interest rates by 25 basis points, so that the rate of re-financing within the Eurozone rose to 4 per cent at the end of 2007. The volatility of that summer, however, soon prompted a more active response on the part of the ECB, as this supposed 'significant worldwide market correction' proceeded to affect liquidity in the Euro money market. The collapse of three BNP Paribas funds provided the catalyst for the beginnings of the unprecedented 'heroic' intervention of the central bank. The result was an initial injection of €95bn on 9 August, swiftly followed by further amounts over the coming days, in a move which was initially criticised by the Bank of England as potentially encouraging excessive risk-taking by financial institutions (*Financial Times*, 2007). Nonetheless, as Northern Rock and two German banks (IKB and Sachsen LB) ran into funding difficulties shortly after, the unprecedented activity of the ECB became somewhat the norm, as it provided liquidity in dollars to the Federal Reserve Bank of New York, and further 'special liquidity measures' in a vain attempt to avert the impending 'credit crunch' (ECB, 2007).

By October radical stabilisation efforts were also being accompanied by a more reflexive and assertive European response. The financial turmoil of 2007 focused attention on improving transparency in financial markets and the regulation of credit rating agencies (CRAs) as well as strengthening the calls for supranational regulation (*Financial Times*, 2007). During earlier EU negotiations (2000–2001) such proposals had been dismissed because of a lack of political will (see Lamfalussy, 2001). Yet, by the ECOFIN (Economic and Financial Affairs Council) meeting on 9 October the emerging theme was for far greater cooperation and regulatory coordination given the degree of interconnectedness of financial systems and the extent of the cross-border operations of the large financial institutions that were presently in trouble (ECOFIN, 2007). Indeed, this agenda echoed research from within the financial services community itself, highlighting the 'incompleteness' of the regulatory architectures, with the European

DOI: 10.1057/9781137298010

Capital Markets Institute neatly capturing this renewed political momentum by stating that 'concerted action is needed involving monetary policy authorities, policy-makers and supervisors to agree on a set of policy priorities and to prepare a more integrated response to crises. The reputation of Europe's financial market is at stake' (Lannoo, 2007; Deutsche Bank, 2007). The crisis had already begun to crystallise an embryonic political consensus, coalescing around the neoliberal mindworld.

As we shall see, aside from financial regulation this embryonic vision had a clear Germanic influence. In particular, it reflected the decisive intervention of the German state in the early 2000s. The Agenda 2010 reforms to the domestic economy marked the decisive attempt by the German state to overcome what it saw as the intransigence of labour unions, in the interests of renewed capital accumulation (Bruff, 2010, pp.415–416). The controversial welfare and labour-market reforms effectively re-focused training assistance towards short- rather than long-term programmes, reduced income-related unemployment benefits, and made mini-jobs (or 'casual' labour) more attractive through tax breaks (ibid.). This radical (neoliberal) re-organisation of capitalist social relations was a direct challenge to the (democratic) mechanisms of consensus-building and the 'collective interests of organized labour' (Upchurch, et al., 2009, p.69) to 'render the country an attractive site for investment and production' (Menz, 2005, p.199). The cruel irony, of course, was that during the period 2003–2007 Germany, though struggling with the burdens of re-unification, was nonetheless becoming more competitive; whilst other countries enjoyed housing and consumption booms on the back of cheap credit, making them less competitive (Soros, 2012). We should bear both the character and consequences of these German reforms in mind as we consider what took place through the course of 2008–2009.

That said, the outlook for the European economy remained relatively positive at the dawn of 2008. The ECB concluded, for example, in its annual report marking the ten-year anniversary of EMU, that since annual inflation had averaged only slightly above 2 per cent,

> this success is tangible proof of the institutional robustness, coherence and unity of the Eurosystem – of its capacity to act in a truly European spirit on the basis of shared values, high standards and common principles. *From the outset, the Euro has been a stable currency.* (ECB, 2008a, p.10, *emphasis added*)

These conclusions were perhaps a little premature, since by June and July HICP inflation peaked at 4 per cent, despite a short-term fall in commodity energy prices, prompting the Bank to raise its key interest rates in July 2008. The devastation of the autumn period was nonetheless still unforeseen.

Though the extraordinary events of September 2008, and the bankruptcy of a leading global financial institution (Lehman Brothers), may have originated in the US markets it is now widely recognised that their impact on European banking was also immense. From 28 September onwards, a host of European financial institutions came under intense market pressure because of perceptions of poor underlying asset quality or of liquidity and capital shortages. Although Euro-area large and complex banking groups (LCBGs) had initially proved relatively resilient to the market fluctuations of 2007, by November 2008 their total writedowns amounted to €73.2 bn (ECB, 2008b, pp.11–13). As a corollary effect, the funding positions of these LCBGs declined and this too added further pressure to the already impaired interbank money market, making liquidity increasingly scarce. The result was a drop of almost €200bn in the market capitalisation of Euro area LCBGs between mid-September and late November.[1]

What was notable at this time was the fact that the responses were predominantly national in origin and design. In particular, this reflected the fact that, after the bankruptcy of Lehman Brothers, Angela Merkel promptly declared that the virtual guarantees extended to other financial institutions should be organised on a country-by-country basis, rather than by designating a central mechanism at the European level. The result was a piecemeal approach that only panicked investors still further (Der Spiegel, 2008). Within 48 hours (starting on 28 September), Belgian, Dutch and Luxembourg authorities, in coordination with ECB president Jean-Claude Trichet, invested €11.2bn in Fortis (Belgium's biggest bank) to save it from an anticipated run on 29 September. The British government also convinced Spanish bank Santander to purchase Bradford & Bingley's £22bn of savings, with the state taking on £41bn of mortgages. Meanwhile, the German government orchestrated an (initial) €35bn bailout of Hypo Real Estate (Europe's largest mortgage lender) involving a consortium of banks, whilst Dexia (the Belgo-French mutual lender) required an injection of €6bn by the Belgian and French governments (see Der Spiegel, 2008; *The Guardian*, 2008).

These individualised national responses provide a useful counterpoint for the European consensus on a banking union that began to emerge in 2012. Yet the impact of September's financial tsunami on

DOI: 10.1057/9781137298010

policy coordination was also immediately obvious. On Monday, 6 October 2008, the Eurogroup ministers met to discuss the unfolding crisis, followed by an ECOFIN Council meeting on 7 October to negotiate a coordinated response to the shocks. Though recognising the different starting conditions of member states' economies, the Council emphasised the need for concerted and coordinated action (ECOFIN, 2008). Initially this began with a reactionary response to the revealed deficiencies of existing regulatory arrangements. On 8 October the Commission established a high-level working group, chaired by former IMF director Jacques de Larosière, to review European supervision of globally operating financial institutions. The significance of this initiative was not overlooked because, whereas the 2001 Lamfalussy Process had stopped short of a supranational regulatory architecture because of remaining national opposition, the de Larosière committee was specifically tasked with assessing the potential for further EU-level supervision. In his speech to the European Parliament on 8 October, Commission President Jose Barroso emphasised that in addressing the crisis 'it makes sense to remove the mismatch between a continental-scale market and national systems of supervision' (Barroso, 2008). EU institutions were not simply concerned with facilitating a talking shop between national regulators, but also to develop and strengthen the European-level apparatus that emerged from the wreckage of the crash. Just as capital is re-structured during times of sustained economic crisis, so 'the scale-configurations upon which it is grounded are likewise reconfigured to create a new geographical scaffolding for a new wave of capitalist growth' (Brenner, 1999, p.434; Macartney and Shields, 2011).

Beyond the European Economic Recovery Plan

Aside from the financial-regulatory agenda, the political momentum for neoliberal reform generated by the crisis was also apparent from the outset. In close parallel to the re-regulatory impetus, a marked degree of multilateral coordination about the stabilisation measures would subsequently give rise to the most important EU-level measure to emerge from this early phase: the European Economic Recovery Plan (EERP). This is perhaps indicative of the fact that, despite comparative differences – perceptible synchronically at various moments of the crisis, and diachronically within each of the member states themselves – there is a clear correlation between the peaks of market panic and the forging of a consensus. The result was another example of state managers exploiting the unfolding crisis as an opportunity to drive reform forward (Cammack, 2009, p.1).

The lead-up to the – coordinated and counter-cyclical – European Economic Recovery Plan (EERP) was precipitated by the transition from banking crisis to a slowdown in the real economy. Informally proposed by the Commission on the 29 October, the EERP was formally outlined on 26 November. In one respect, however, the EERP was little more than the sum total of the individual stimulus packages declared by member states for 2009, with the EU only urging more reluctant member states to pursue the necessary measures (Commission, 2008b); it amounted to €200bn and included only €30bn from the EU Commission. The first strand of the EERP therefore reflected the extant stabilisation efforts of national governments.

But beyond the assemblage of these (and similar) national initiatives the European Economic Recovery Plan also marked the entrepreneurship of the Commission as it pressed for renewed emphasis on implementing Lisbon II structural reforms (Interview BAFIN, 2011; Interview Commission, 2011). In the November proposal the Commission framed this as a second pillar, aimed at reinforcing Europe's competitiveness in the long term. This shifted the emphasis from simply mitigating the human cost of the economic downturn in terms of stemming the loss of jobs and focused on the return to growth through counter-cyclical spending and 'priority actions, grounded in the Lisbon Strategy' (Commission, 2008b, pp.2, 6).

As yet, however, this political project was only partially gestated. This meant that the mix of revenue and expenditure instruments proposed (in the short-term) tended to simply reflect the policy decisions of the Franco-German axis, with a more emphatic shift towards budgetary discipline, a feature of later policies. The EERP suggested that 'discretionary public spending is considered to have a stronger positive impact on demand in the short-run compared with tax cuts', though lower social contributions would aid job retention whilst lower taxation could support labour purchasing power (Commission, 2009a, p.19). Yet the renewal of the neoliberal project was apparent as the Commission spoke of structural reforms necessary to address the underlying *root causes* of the crisis. They emphasised the disparity between wage-setting mechanisms and productivity in certain countries, the lack of flexibility

DOI: 10.1057/9781137298010

of labour-market arrangements which had left them ill-equipped to deal with the demand disturbances of such a crisis, and also the reduction of barriers to entrepreneurship – whether by creating openings for the low-skilled or enhancing access to financing for business. The parallels with their comments from 2006 were stark. An increase in competition, establishment of an attractive economic environment for international capital, and a deepening of the rule of market discipline over labour power, all these therefore formed the overarching vision; and the strategic targeting of spaces and enclaves previously under-exposed to these imperatives became the next priority after stabilisation. The EERP was finally approved by the European Council at their session on 11–12 December 2008.

One distinguishing feature of the unfolding crisis has been its ability to generate unforeseen conditions. The relationship with political agency is therefore no simple, linear, causal one whereby state managers respond to exogenous pressures because neoliberal structural reform and depoliticisation are the only alternative. Instead, in Polanyi's words 'such groups are pushing that which is falling and holding onto that which, under its own steam, is moving their way. It may then seem as if they had originated the process of social change, while actually they were merely its beneficiaries, and may even be perverting the trend to make it serve their own aims' (1957, p.28). This was clearly the case from the start of 2009, as the instability of the previous year turned into a 'rapid and synchronised fall in economic activity worldwide', or a Great Recession (ECB, 2009a, p.10). With the 'limits' of deficit-financed stimulus packages soon to become apparent, the struggle for economic growth would prove to be the furnace in which the doctrine of austerity was (re-)forged. Here democratic demands and the remaining 'privileges' of the welfare state would come under systematic and sustained attack.

Nonetheless, it would be wrong to underplay the sheer scale of the slump experienced in 2009; to do so would risk ascribing an undue rationality, coherence and intent to state managers in the crystallisation and implementation of the ordo/neo-liberal project. Indeed, though Euro area real GDP contracted by 4 per cent, the recession(s) ranged from around 2 per cent in France to almost 5 per cent in Germany, Italy and the UK, and around 7–7.5 per cent in Slovenia, Ireland and Finland, with those of the Baltic region even more severe – 14 per cent in Estonia and 18 per cent in Latvia and Lithuania (Commission, 2009b, p.8). Essentially, the variations tended to reflect three variables: the size of the financial sector (and exposure to risky assets), the export dependency of the economy, and the extent to which house prices had been overvalued. Yet the realisation of 2007 – that Europe was not insulated against the crash in US sub-prime markets – was now compounded by the fact that the challenge to the European economy would be severe.

In France, the predominance of retail banking left the economy in a somewhat more insulated position than its neighbours. Yet it still experienced a tightening in lending and liquidity, and was hit by the fall in world trade (Commission, 2009b, p. 99; INSEE, 2010, pp.7, 9, 12). Though not especially export-oriented, two-thirds of its exports went to the European Union, which made it particularly susceptible to the recession of 2009. As a result GDP fell by 2.2 per cent, a fall which – though less steep than its neighbouring economies and the Euro area as a whole – was still marked. The relatively large size of the public sector, the small degree of openness, and the size of the manufacturing sector played a stabilising role in this regard, but also created a different set of problems thus slowing the recovery. Together, the toll on French public finances was marked, with the debt to GDP ratio rising to approximately 85 per cent by 2010 compared to close to 70 per cent at the end of 2008.

There were also other countries whose openness and export-orientation undermined previously relatively strong positions. Finland, for example, had benefited from a decade of export-driven growth and had built up substantial surpluses in the current account and government finances. Initially affected by a fall in consumer confidence, the most dramatic impact came as Finnish exports dropped by the greatest percentage in the Euro area (Commission, 2009b, p.147). Most significantly, the appreciation of the Euro's exchange rate against that of Finland's main trading partners – given that over 70 per cent of its exports go outside the Euro area – was devastating for the Finnish economy. The Finnish surplus in public finances, however, meant that the state was able to provide for a relatively large fiscal stimulus (1.5 per cent of GDP in 2009 and a further 1 per cent in 2010) focused primarily on tax cuts (such as personal income tax). Yet the result was that government finances fell by over 7 percentage points to a deficit of 3 per cent in 2009, and with relatively high wage-increase commitments and the medium to long-term loss of external-price competitiveness Finland faced a prolonged period of adjustment.

Peripheral countries on the other hand faced almost insurmountable difficulties. Government borrowing costs began to climb dramatically

DOI: 10.1057/9781137298010

from mid-January, as yield spreads relative to the German Bund widened. This prompted a downgrading of the long-term credit ratings for Greek, Portuguese and Spanish sovereign debt which then only compounded the widening spreads (Commission, 2009c, p.6). For Ireland, decade-long growth came to an end with the adjustment from its 2006 peak, starting in the housing market and spreading to the wider economy (Commission, 2009b, p.89). The decline in global demand subsequently impacted trade, whilst the relative weight of the financial sector and its banks' high dependence on foreign wholesale finance also hit Ireland hard. GDP growth correspondingly fell by 3 per cent in 2008. As public finances deteriorated still further, domestic demand was impacted by a significant fall in employment and nominal wage declines. The difficulty then for Ireland was that, with the need to consolidate public finances, there was less recourse to public investment. State managers therefore also instituted a series of tax-increasing measures throughout 2009, to moderate the effects of the revenue decline coupled with capital expenditure cuts announced in the April 2009 supplementary budget. As we shall see in later chapters, this toxic mix only exacerbated the challenges of selective intervention – to restore profitable accumulation whilst rejecting demands for increased social spending – for Irish state managers.

Spain fitted a similar pattern, with decade-long economic expansion coming to an end in the second half of 2008. Again, external imbalances, a high degree of household indebtedness, an oversized housing sector, and the persistent loss of competitiveness had led to an adjustment of the economy from 2007 (Commission, 2009b, pp.95, 97). The downturn (a fall of 3.75 per cent in 2009) took a heavy toll on both public finances and jobs. The Spanish government responded with a fiscal stimulus – to support households and businesses – of around 2.5 per cent of GDP. In terms of long-term structural reform however, EU institutions were swift to note the fact that nominal wages had been slow in responding to changing labour-market conditions, while job losses and unemployment were sharply rising. Hence the disconnection between wages and productivity developments was a major factor undermining the competitive position of the Spanish economy. Moreover, as the downturn negatively affected tax intensity and significantly increased social protection needs, falling revenue-to-GDP and rising expenditure-to-GDP ratios also adversely affected public accounts in 2009. Again, the emergence of new social movements in Spain – such as the *Indignados* – was a direct consequence of these events (see Chapter 4).

DOI: 10.1057/9781137298010

Greece too ended a decade of (on paper) strong economic growth with a recession that began in 2009. There were already concerns though, about the reliability of Greek financial accounting and the weakness of public finances which had placed Greece on the Stability and Growth Pact excessive deficit radar prior to the start of the crisis itself. We will consider these factors in greater detail below. Suffice it to note that persistent long-term domestic and external imbalances were accelerated by the unfolding crisis, with government debt-financing proving increasingly expensive, putting further pressure on the already strained budget.

Portugal was therefore somewhat different, having posted weak economic growth below the Euro area average since the early 2000s. This was characterised by low productivity, poor competitiveness, a sizeable external deficit, and rising unemployment (4 per cent in 2000 and 7.8 per cent by 2008) (OECD, 2011; Commission, 2009b, p.135). The crisis only compounded already problematic conditions, with GDP contracting by nearly 3 per cent in 2009. So the Portuguese state was limited in its policy options, initially implementing discretionary measures to stimulate the economy, whilst also pursuing substantive structural reforms. The fiscal stimulus – focused on public investment, social protection and support to employment, investment and exports by the private sector – amounted to approximately 1.25 per cent of GDP in 2009. Nonetheless, the government deficit rose to 8 per cent of GDP in 2009, from 2.7 per cent in 2008 (Commission, 2009b, p.137).

In Germany, however, events would unfold that would in turn reshape the very course of the crisis. Though its large export-oriented manufacturing sector and its specialisation in investment goods had made it particularly exposed to the global trade shock, the economy returned to positive real GDP growth in the second quarter of 2009 (Commission, 2009b, pp.82–84). The system of guarantees to stabilise the banking system (the Financial Market Stabilisation Fund) and the fiscal stimulus aided the speed of the recovery, as did the shift to flexible working arrangements implemented at the peak of the crisis. But this was also a product of pre-crisis labour-market reforms and wage moderation (see above), which further cushioned the German economy against experiencing more dramatic rises in unemployment.

Arguably the key to understanding Germany's zeal for the EU's subsequent austerity programme, and its 'first-mover' advantage, can be traced back to a constitutional reform in June 2009. Little noticed by the outside world, it imposed a structural deficit ceiling of 0.35 per cent of

DOI: 10.1057/9781137298010

GDP for the Federal government as of 2016. It came as a response to the rise in debt levels from 66 per cent of GDP in 2008 to a forecasted 80 per cent by 2011. Yet the impact of this unilateral move captured the 'first, second and third priority of German economic policy': deficit reduction in the name of sound money (Munchau, 2009).

In essence, it was a distinctly political move to further *depoliticise* fiscal policy. By anchoring the new stability law in the national constitution, only a two-thirds majority would be able to undo it. Instead, future fiscal policy would be in the hands of Germany's Constitutional Court. The aim, beyond slashing public debt and ensuring that Germany never again 'strays from the path of virtue', was to buttress markets' confidence in Germany' (*The Economist*, 2011b). Three key features are worth noting: the first was that it replaced an already existing, albeit softer, constitutional clause – that deficits can only be used to finance investments. It seemed that the softer mechanism had not prevented public debt from climbing, so the *Schuldenbremse* (balanced budget amendment) sought to send 'a clear signal to market participants and underpin confidence and long term expectations' (Federal Ministry of Finance, 2009, p.3; *The Economist*, 2011b). The second component was that it established a detailed statistical toolkit to implement the rules over the economic cycle. Both of these features would later re-appear in the European frame, leading the IMF to conclude that this was a 'remarkable political achievement' given that 'the focus of political opinion is still in most countries on crisis recovery and not on fiscal consolidation' (IMF, 2009b).

The third feature, however, was perhaps even more important, as the timing of efforts to meet the deficit criteria would prove to be crucial. If Germany were unable to return to growth by 2011 then the new law would produce a pro-cyclical fiscal policy, leaving Germany in a downward spiral that threatened the Eurozone. On the other hand, if Germany resumed growth the consolidation phase would effectively begin in a cyclical upturn. Germany would only benefit from the new law however, if – alongside the existing Lisbon II structural reform agenda – other member states too began a period of deficit reduction. The irony here, of course, was that Germany's export-dependent economy would rely on deficit-led recoveries in its main trading partners. As one commentator therefore opined, the 'balanced budget constitutional law [was] not about economics. It [was] a moral crusade' intended to forcibly compel all Eurozone members towards consolidation (Munchau, 2009). This would soon become all too apparent.

DOI: 10.1057/9781137298010

Indeed, whilst coordinated measures to address the liquidity constraints across the Union continued, the molecular shift towards fiscal consolidation, the intensification of pressures to implement neoliberal structural reform, and the crystallisation of centralised institutional resolve to drive reform forward, gathered pace. Initially this was less obvious, masked by an extensive programme of EU investment: €3.1bn in Community financial assistance to Latvia on 3 February; €100 million to the Western Balkans and €5.5 million (for the Globalisation Adjustment Fund) to support the 1300 German workers at Nokia (31 July); €39 million for Bosnia and Herzegovina (11th August); €200 million to Serbia (8 October) and further aid to Armenia and Georgia (16 October). Yet, already, the EU aid to Latvia was tied to agreements in line with the Economic Stabilization and Growth Programme for structural reforms.[2] This was, of course, reminiscent of the conditionality 'perfected' by the IMF after the Third World debt crisis, though it marked the forging of a nascent consensus in the management of this most recent crisis (European Community, 2009; see also Shields, 2007).

By the Eurogroup and ECOFIN meetings (9–10 February 2009) and G7 meeting in Rome (13–14 February) this consensus – that neoliberal, 'growth enhancing' measures must accompany short-term stimulus efforts – was garnering support (IMF 2009c). Specifically, these growth-enhancing measures took the form of restoring the stability of budgetary positions and began (18 February) with the Commission assessing the Stability and Convergence Programmes of: the 11 countries (Bulgaria, the Czech Republic, Denmark, Germany, Estonia, Hungary, the Netherlands, Poland, Sweden, Finland and the United Kingdom) with budget deficits at that time within the 3 per cent limits of the Stability and Growth Pact; and then another group of six countries (Ireland, Greece, Spain, France, Latvia and Malta) which had breached the 3 per cent reference value (Commission, 2009d). Indeed, messages of budgetary consolidation began to emerge from the IMF as 2009 unfolded (IMF, 2009d; 2009e), and were reinforced by a slowly re-invigorated set of ratings agencies (Forbes, 2009; *Irish Times*, 2009).[3]

Indeed, the timing of austerity clearly reflected the growing concerns of capital that state managers might again succumb to discretionary social spending to contain the demands of nascent protest movements. In January 2009 for instance, Spain, Ireland and Greece were all warned by Standard & Poors that their ratings were under threat. The point was that for large institutional investors – who, incidentally make their

DOI: 10.1057/9781137298010

money from 'market-making and transactions, rather than loans and investments' and had recovered rather quickly from the 2008 crash – prolonged deficit-financing had long been stigmatised as threatening price stability (Radice, 2011, p.130); and despite the irony that a major part of the deficits had been incurred in rescuing the banking system they were still keen on re-asserting the common sense of tight budgetary discipline, and avoiding the temptation to incur further public debt through Keynesian-style social spending. Behind the emerging political agenda therefore lay a stark reality infused with class relations.

Throughout the first quarter this agenda gathered momentum, with the Commission issuing a Communication entitled 'Driving European Recovery' on 4 March. The report marked the beginnings of 'action ... which targets efforts on the long-term objective of building a competitive and sustainable EU economy, as set out in the Lisbon strategy for Growth and Jobs' (Commission, 2009e, p.2). Yet it was the specific targeting of excessive budget deficits incurred during the crisis – 'budget deficits should return to positions consistent with the need to ensure long-term sustainability of public finances as soon as economic conditions allow' – and the need to 'combine an immediate stimulus with the long-term perspective [required] ... to meet the challenges of a world economy' that characterised the second wave of the EU response (ibid., pp.9–10). Price stability and 'sound money' had to be restored at all costs. Indeed, from 24 March the Commission proceeded to act upon this (re)new(ed) perspective, taking formal steps to address the deficits of Greece, Spain, France and Ireland, which exceeded the Stability and Growth Pact (SGP) values, whilst revising its recommendations for the UK. Importantly, it cited Council Regulation 1466/97 (ratified in 1997) to emphasise that the temporary suspension of fiscal stringency during the immediate crash had now passed.

In turn, this message gradually began to effuse from the corridors of the EU institutions. At the Brussels Economic Forum, 14–15 May, for example, European Commissioner Joaquín Almunia captured this sentiment, stating

> At this juncture, immediate crisis response is our first priority. And yet, in our efforts to manage current challenges, we must take a longer term perspective. Deep crises leave a lasting trace on economic activity. They bring powerful lessons for economic governance ... Already now, [we must ask] how do we plan for the unwinding of the economic recovery plans and withdrawal of the massive support to the banking sector when growth and

DOI: 10.1057/9781137298010

stability return?...Medium term economic performance depends a great deal on action taken during a crisis. (Almunia, 2009)

By June the Commission Report on Public Finances focused specifically on the ratcheting up of the public debt-to-GDP ratio which was projected to rise from 58.7 per cent in 2007 to an expected 79.4 per cent of GDP by 2010 (Commission, 2009a, pp.2, 5, 7–8). The Report therefore addressed the need for credible exit strategies and better economic governance mechanisms aimed at the surveillance of public finances.

In essence, this became a question of balancing the timing and scale of the withdrawal of budgetary support, consolidating budgets, and introducing structural reforms to replace the supposedly artificial 'propping-up' effect of state aid and address productivity gaps. Beyond these economic considerations, however, this involved a very real political calculation of responding to the demands of capital (withdrawal and reform) without further exacerbating the simmering discontent of subaltern social groups; again, steady and intelligent seemed the best option. As we shall see in the following chapters, the political management of this struggle has proven to be a relatively elusive task, with recourse to a more authoritarian and depoliticised politics the only solution (see Commission, 2009f, p.iii; ECOFIN, 2009a, p.6; 2009b). Yet this too is consistent with neoliberalism which, on the hand, operates under the rubric of 'free markets liberated from state interference', whilst in practice entailing 'a dramatic intensification of coercive, disciplinary forms of state intervention to impose market rule upon all aspects of social life' (Brenner and Theodore, 2002, p.5).

Summary

This chapter began with the crises of legitimacy and debt confronting the EU. By tracing through the cataclysmic events of the first phase of the crisis this chapter has sought to flesh out the claim that, from very early on, state managers began to recognise the unique opportunity that was presenting itself. Inertia and sluggish progress had characterised the implementation of Lisbon reforms in the 2000s. The financial crisis and great recession could effectively galvanise political resolve and synergise efforts to address remaining productivity gaps and competitiveness imbalances, re-structuring social relations in favour of capital. The EU,

DOI: 10.1057/9781137298010

like all good institutions, understood a fundamental truth: that the right time to reform is always now. As Stuart Shields notes, 'when times are good, abundant social resources are available to fund reforms; when times are bad, crisis weakens resistance and justifies reform' (Shields, 2012, p.18). Moreover, this feeds into a narrative constructing the crisis as the product of *insufficient* reforms, rather than the logical conclusion of the actual trajectory of past reforms.[4]

Indeed, this is perhaps the obvious but all-important point to note: it was not simply the lack of an alternative paradigm that precipitated the renewal of neoliberal reforms; it was the particular fusion of a long-gestated neoliberal ideology and the crystallisation – further fuelled by the crisis itself – of a consensus among state managers to implement structural reform and austerity. This is why the political responses to the crisis must be seen as the extension and intensification of the European project to 'inscribe the neoliberal policy of market freedom associated with Hayek through the creation of constitutional devices associated with [German] ordo-liberalism' (Bonefeld, 1998, p.67).

Though the reaction by the demos would only gather pace in 2010 – requiring additional political management – the question of further insulating the policymaking apparatus from the distortionary effects of democratic influence implicitly framed these early efforts by the political classes. As the debt crisis began to unfold in 2010, pressures from both international financial markets and the European electorate would provide the critical imperatives for stronger and more centralised statecraft. The second phase of the crisis would bring with it the shift towards constructing the right kind of (depoliticised) institutions to buttress renewed accumulation and, it was hoped, dispel resistance by emphasising the economic necessity of such measures.

Notes

1   In comparative terms, International Monetary Fund (IMF) figures indicate that between 2007 and 2010 US banks lost 8 per cent ($1,025bn) of their total holdings for loans and securities in writedowns, UK banks lost 7 per cent ($604bn), Euro area banks 5 per cent ($201bn), and Asian banks also lost 5 per cent ($166bn) (IMF, 2009, pp.10–11).

2   Aid to Latvia was provided in conjunction with an IMF loan of €1.7bn, €1.9bn from Nordic countries (Sweden, Denmark, Norway, Finland, and

Estonia), and €0.4bn from the European Bank for Reconstruction and Development, the Czech Republic and Poland.

3   In January 2009, for instance, Spain, Ireland and Greece were all warned by Standard & Poors that their ratings were under threat. This was somewhat ironic, given the shaming ratings agencies had received for their role in the earlier sub-prime debacle.

4   See, for example, the Spring European Council agenda, emphasising the need for member states to return to medium-term budgetary objectives; and the need to pursue and *accelerate* structural reforms, all of which were deemed central to attractiveness of the European economy to transnational capital. (European Council, 2009).

DOI: 10.1057/9781137298010

3
From Debt Crisis to Depoliticisation

Abstract: *This chapter charts the second phase, as the debt crisis began to grip Europe. It shows how the focus rapidly changed from structural reform to primarily being targeted at restoring budget discipline and sound money. It shows how this drive began in Germany with the constitutional reform of 2009 and transitioned into renewed depoliticisation at the European level.*

Macartney, Huw. *The Debt Crisis and European Democratic Legitimacy*. Basingstoke: Palgrave Macmillan, 2013. DOI: 10.1057/9781137298010.

The previous chapter argued that democratic discussion was not simply a temporary casualty of the period 2007–2009 as is often suggested at times of heightened threats to national security. Instead, amidst the intense bricolage of early efforts at counter-cyclical spending and tighter financial regulation, a previously germinated neoliberal ideology gave shape to a (re-)nascent project for Europe. As such, state managers sought to exploit the crisis as an opportunity to drive forward structural reform that had previously faced opposition as it came into confrontation with vestiges of the democratic-welfare state. Neoliberal reform had also, earlier, relied largely upon domestic elites who had lacked the required capacities. The crisis therefore also provoked efforts to strengthen supra-national institutional architectures.

Traces of this project were evident from as early as 2008, and began condensing into a reinvigorated austerity agenda and new, more coercive, institutions from the start of 2009. Importantly however, there was also evidence of the seeds of both the debt crisis and the German recovery (and future leadership) through this early period. In an unanticipated turn of events the interplay between the movements of international financial markets, the responses of the European demos, an emergent coalition of Franco-German, and 'forward-thinking' EU state managers would come to shape the course of the crisis from 2010.

The Greek debt catalyst

One thing is clear amidst the mindboggling and constantly changing complexities of the last few years: that the degree of integration of the European economy – its financial and production systems in particular – has only added to the pace of the shift from one phase of the crisis to another. Though EU institutions began 2010 with a set of strategies formulated through the course of 2009, the headlines were grabbed by the rapidly unfolding sovereign debt crisis. This meant returning to fire-fighting and bricolage, attempting to placate international bond markets whilst simultaneously seeking to contain the spillover of national protests at the deficit reduction (austerity) measures.

On 14 October 2009 the Commission had issued its Communication on the Long-Term Sustainability of Public Finances, with the following ECOFIN meeting (19–20 October) indicating that, dependent on further signs of economic recovery, fiscal consolidation should begin in

DOI: 10.1057/9781137298010

all member states by 2011 at the latest (Commission, 2009g; ECOFIN, 2009a). Yet by 9 December the EU's strategy was seemingly already under siege as financial markets and ratings agencies expressed concerns over the sustainability of Greece's public finances (Reuters, 2009). This was not unexpected, given that between July 2004 and June 2007 Greece had been subject to the Council's excessive deficit procedure, with notice of insufficient progress being issued in 2005 under Treaty Article 104(9). In fact, however, Eurostat had raised the problem of Greece presenting false economic data on numerous occasions from as early as 2002, when Greek authorities had to admit that they had entered EMU under false pretences (Schelkle, 2010, p. 16). In sum, high government deficits, rapidly increasing government debt-to-GDP ratios and rising contingent liabilities on account of guarantees for banks sent yields spiralling (ECB, 2010a, pp. 21–22). Spreads for ten-year government bonds of some Euro-area countries relative to German government bonds started to increase rapidly, reaching unprecedented levels by May 2010.

As 2010 began, Eurostat released a further report (11 January 2010) which questioned the reliability of Greek statistics. Put simply, on 2 and 21 October 2009 Greek authorities had submitted two different sets of Excessive Deficit Procedure notification tables to EU authorities covering the government deficit and debt data for 2005–2008, and a forecast for 2009. In the 21 October notification, the Greek government deficit for 2008 was revised from 5.0 per cent of GDP (the ratio reported by Greece, and published and validated by Eurostat in April 2009) to 7.7 per cent of GDP. At the same time, the Greek authorities also revised the planned deficit ratio for 2009 from 3.7 per cent of GDP (the figure reported in spring) to 12.5 per cent of GDP (Commission, 2010a, p. 3). As was noted earlier though, Greek accounting failures alone do not account for the structural imbalances which underpinned the weaknesses of peripheral countries. This was therefore not simply a failure on the part of the EU to begin the deficit cutting measures early enough, but the accumulation of the contradictions of the European project itself. The fact that international markets were now preparing to 'discipline' these peripheral states for their 'profligacy' – incidentally, in a move that reinforces the methodological nationalism of contemporary views of the crisis – only added to the irony.[1]

Faced with growing tensions the Greek government submitted its Stability Programme for 2010–2013 to the European Commission on 15 January. The plan was to reduce the budget deficit to 8.7 per cent of GDP

DOI: 10.1057/9781137298010

in 2010 and thereafter to 5.6 per cent in 2011, 2.8 per cent in 2012 and 2 per cent in 2013. Already the programme was radical in its scope: it proposed the elimination of tax exemptions; the rise of excise duties on tobacco and alcohol; as well as measures to fight tax evasion. Beyond that, the government planned to reduce expenditure by cutting public servant allowances; freezing recruitment in 2010 and reducing the number of civil servants recruited to replace future retirees by 80 per cent; freezing all budgetary appropriations per government ministry by 10 per cent; and adopting nominal cuts in public consumption and operational expenditure (Commission, 2010b). The programme also outlined a number of structural reforms aimed at improving the budgetary framework and the efficiency of public spending, enhancing investment and improving the functioning of labour and product markets. Under article 121(4) of the Union Treaty, however, the Commission recommended to the European Council that an even more comprehensive structural reform package be agreed, in order to maintain the 'consistency and functioning of the monetary union itself', and urged Greece to cut its overall wage bill.[2] This was also supplemented by a recommendation under article 126(9) giving notice of the need for *immediate* deficit reduction measures and launching an 'infringement procedure' against Greek authorities for their failure to report reliable budgetary statistics (Commission, 2010c).

The significance of this act was monumental: this was the first time that the budgetary and economic surveillance instruments foreseen in the Treaty were used 'simultaneously and in an integrated way' (ibid.). The recommendations were subsequently endorsed by the ECOFIN Council on 15–16 February, in collaboration with experts from the ECB and IMF, in what was an 'impossibly stringent and intrusive' budgetary adjustment programme (Schelke, 2010, p.16; ECOFIN, 2010a). The point was simple: EU institutions were beginning to recognise the transmission mechanisms which could translate this (seemingly) isolated crisis of sovereign debt into a crisis for the single currency area. Yet this next phase of the crisis also reflected an awareness that incurring large debts to salvage the financial system was exacerbating the EU's existing legitimacy crisis (see Chapter 4).

As a direct result, the Greek public came out in protest against the austerity measures, with customs and tax officials holding a one-day strike on 4 February followed by a one-day general strike on 24 February (*The Guardian*, 2010a). The strike also coincided with the visit of the so-called 'troika' of EU, ECB and IMF experts to Athens to assess the state of Greek finances, delivering a grim assessment which only aggravated tensions. Greek Prime Minister Papandreou captured the emergent neo-liberal consensus though and on the required course of action, he suggested that 'Our duty today is to forget about the political cost and think only about the survival of our country. Past policies make it necessary to proceed to *brutal changes and reduce accumulated privileges*' (*emphasis added The Telegraph*, 2010). The early public alarm of Septembers 2007 and 2008 had subsided. Now, as electorates began coming to terms with the grim realities of austerity, earlier state interventions to salvage banking systems were morphing into a more sustained and comprehensive attack on the remaining vestiges of social policy.

Austerity

Predictably, the next round of Greek cuts brought with it the next round of public protests (11 March), yet the crystallising consensus amongst state managers continued to gain momentum, with ECOFIN approving the latest measures on 15–16 March. The most important development during this period though was the beginning of the downward debt spiral that would come to undermine the 'benefits' of austerity. Put differently, the explicit rationale behind austerity was to re-assure international markets that 'high and unsustainable' deficits (and, by extension, prolonged public involvement) would be tackled. In so doing the costs of borrowing would fall as investment and output responded favourably. In principle this mirrored the logic of the German constitutional amendment and the EU recommendations of early 2009. Yet, as Greek PM Papandreou addressed the European Parliament's Special Committee on the Economic, Political and Social Crisis (18 March) it was becoming apparent that the austerity-for-growth plan wasn't working: since borrowing costs had not fallen Greece would soon be unable to sustain deficit reduction (Papandreou, 2010a). Instead, austerity had a second and subtler social function: it constituted a golden opportunity to smash heavily entrenched class compromises and 'dysfunctional' institutions.[3]

In light of Greece's difficulties, the European Council meeting on 25–26 March led to the establishment of an emergency mechanism, in spite of intergovernmental tensions and opposition from French and German finance ministers. The mechanism was comprised of coordinated bilateral loans (from Member States) and European and IMF funding,

DOI: 10.1057/9781137298010

calculated at €30bn at non-concessional interest rates of 5 per cent (Council, 2010a). Moreover, the ECB Governing Council simultaneously decided to throw caution to the wind, extending softer rules on collateral and accepting Greek government bonds regardless of their ratings. These decisions prompted Commission President Barroso to proudly conclude that the EU had 'solved this in the European family', asserting that this was an 'exceptional problem' facing '*one* of our Member States which had been met by a coordinated and decisive EU response' (Barroso, 2010b). The European Council meeting had another, less well-publicised, impact however, and one which was conceived in the chaos of the sovereign debt crisis itself: it began the formal process of exploring how to strengthen the legal framework surrounding the surveillance of economic and budgetary risks (Council, 2010a, p.2). As Papandreou had put it only a week earlier, these were precisely the 'institutions which [were] missing in this project' (Papandreou, 2010b).

Nonetheless, an overview of the events that followed again dispels any overestimation of the rationale and cogency of the political project at work. On 11 April, Euro area heads-of-state and government issued a statement supporting the €30bn loan package, indicating their approval of the Greek government's efforts in the early months of 2010 (Eurogroup, 2010a). Once again, the impact on market spreads was brief (*The Guardian*, 2010b). The final straw was the announcement by Eurostat (22 April) that Greece's budget deficit for 2009 was 13.6 per cent of GDP, as opposed to the 12.7 per cent it had earlier reported (Eurostat, 2010). On 23 April, Greek Prime Minister George Papandreou thus officially requested a €45bn bailout package after borrowing costs soared, rendering funding of the country's large public deficit and debt almost impossible (*The Guardian*, 2010c). Greece had effectively found itself trapped within a vicious downward spiral, as it sought to refinance €16bn of maturing debt by the end of May, and interest rates for borrowing hit a record 8.3 per cent. These disastrous conditions were only compounded by a decision by the ratings agency Moody's to further downgrade Greece's long-term debt rating (*Financial Times*, 2010a). The move for international aid nevertheless enraged both right-wing opposition parties and unions, who claimed that Papandreou was handing 'the keys of the country to the IMF', suggesting that this was 'a premeditated crime against Greek society' (*The Guardian*, 2010d; Bloomberg, 2010).

The bailout was agreed, and the hope of some semblance of calm seemed at least possible. The hope was again short-lived. By 2 May

DOI: 10.1057/9781137298010

it became apparent that the initial package was simply insufficient. Greek government bonds were downgraded to junk status. As a result, Euro members pledged a further €80bn and the IMF another €30bn (Eurogroup, 2010b). Yet the seemingly insurmountable debt crisis was already highlighting the strains both at the national level – between state managers and their electorates – and, resultantly, within the Union itself. In particular, Germany, which was the real linchpin in the entire Euro area salvage operation, was divided over Greek aid, with the government 'stuck in a state between apprehension and self-confidence' (Deutsche Welle, 2010). There was widespread support amongst the German electorate for a return to economic stability and budgetary prudence; but the suggestion that Germany should seemingly sacrifice this objective by footing the bill for spendthrift Greeks was abhorrent. Faced with German intransigence ECB President Trichet and IMF Managing Director Strauss-Kahn made a personal visit to the Bundestag at the end of April, meeting with Finance Minister Wolfgang Schauble and leaders of parliamentary groups, in order to convince them of the urgency of the assistance plan (Der Spiegel, 2010). This was one of those occasions when the entrepreneurship of international elites was pivotal. On Friday 7 May the parliament in Berlin finally approved the country's €22.4bn share of the Greek rescue, the largest of any country.

The following week nonetheless saw some of the most dramatic events in the unfolding debt crisis. Since the bailout on the 2 May, financial markets were driving yields on the bonds of weaker Eurozone governments (in particular, Ireland, Portugal and Spain) to unsustainably high levels, with Standard & Poors (ratings agency) downgrading Portuguese and Spanish bonds accordingly. The severity led to an emergency ECOFIN meeting on the weekend of 8–9 May, with the added pressure of finding a solution before Asian markets opened on Monday morning and the threat becoming potentially cataclysmic for the Euro area as a whole. As one commentator suggested, this was a meeting 'on the edge of the abyss' (Barber, 2010). Indeed, this was the reality which confronted EU and domestic state managers, as they urged the Commission to design a 'stabilisation mechanism' to protect the Eurozone from collapse. Finally, a 'special purpose vehicle' entitled the European Financial Stability Facility (EFSF) totalling €750bn – €60bn in EU funds, €440bn in Eurozone government guarantees, and an additional €250bn in IMF contributions – was proposed by Maarten Verwey, of the Dutch finance ministry. Alongside the dramatic events of August 2011, this set of measures also highlighted the importance of high-pressure circumstances in polarising political views, aiding agreement on the need for more coercive centralised institutions.

Depoliticisation and the strong state

Against the background of the Greek – and later Irish, Italian, Spanish, and Portuguese – travails a more disciplinary and depoliticised institutional apparatus was thus taking shape. At a European Policy Centre conference (15 April 2010) on Reinforcing Economic Governance, European Commissioner Olli Rehn noted that though (at that time) 'the critical test of the worst economic crisis of the last 30 years' had been passed, it had revealed institutional and structural inadequacies: 'Peer pressure has lacked teeth to ensure timely and effective action. Member states did not use the good times to reduce the public debt. Macroeconomic imbalances were neglected.' He suggested that whilst the monetary element of Economic and Monetary Union was strong, less emphasis had been placed on strengthening the economic pillar, since there had been 'no political appetite for action ... until today' (Rehn, 2010a).[4] A formal proposal was thus submitted (12 May 2010) comprising three main building blocks: reinforcing the Stability and Growth Pact (SGP), deepening and broadening economic surveillance, and setting up a permanent crisis resolution mechanism. Yet it was compliance that was seen as the key, because it posed the most immediate threat.

As a result, the Commission proposed to reinforce the preventive and corrective arms of the SGP. In their view, the Excessive Deficit Procedure of the Pact required additional penalties to be imposed on member states flouting the terms. Similarly, they indicated the need to go beyond simply monitoring budgets, by extending surveillance of macroeconomic imbalances and competitiveness divergences. The third element then would extend the ad hoc mechanism into a permanent-resolution mechanism with strong disincentives for activation, making it an instrument of last resort (Commission, 2010d). This was followed shortly after by the establishment of a Task Force on economic governance (21 May) including Mr Van Rompuy as President of the European Council, Finance ministers as representatives of all 27 Member States, Commissioner Olli Rehn, ECB President Jean-Claude Trichet, and Eurogroup President Juncker. The strengthening of supranational tools

DOI: 10.1057/9781137298010

to enforce fiscal discipline, and overcome – by circumventing – domestic obstacles, was now underway.

Importantly, the Commission subsequently issued a more developed report on enhancing coordination on 30 June, which emphasised the social value (read jobs and growth) of its proposed governance reforms (Commission, 2010e). Of course the ordering of priorities was no coincidence, with the social agenda only permissible within the parameters of fiscal discipline. Here the proposals were linked more explicitly to the Europe 2020 strategy – a comprehensive package proposed on 3 March 2010 – which aimed to increase the intensity and pace of product and labour-market reforms, making it the latest stage in the Lisbon agenda (ECB, 2010b, pp.5–7; Commission, 2010f, p.2). The Europe 2020 vision indicated that the 'average potential growth rate over the period 2011–2020 [will] be around 1.5 per cent in the EU27 ... without *bold reforms* ... [and that] This is significantly lower than the rates observed in the EU in the past two decades, which already were much lower than those recorded in the US'.[5] Concerning productivity, it was suggested that the pace of capital accumulation might be slowed by a variety of factors including low global and domestic demand (itself in part due to austerity measures), the need for re-building stocks of capital, and capital costs themselves. The vicious circle this might entail featured prominently in EU assessments, with the crisis resulting in an overall slowdown in industrial re-structuring, caused by either credit constraints (due to adjustments in the banking sector) or by entrenched structural rigidities. Similarly, labour markets threatened to be negatively impacted by the crisis through reductions in average hours worked and in labour participation as well as an increase in the rate of structural unemployment (ibid., pp.48–49). As such, the logic was clear: to up the pace and intensity of neoliberal reform and, cognizant of the forces of resistance which this would provoke, to establish a stronger institutional apparatus at the EU-level that was functionally detached from loci of social conflict.

Specifically, this second communication set out detailed instruments, and transitioned into a formal package of proposals presented on 29 September. These included mechanisms for the surveillance of macroeconomic imbalances, comprising a *preventive* and a *corrective* arm. The preventive arm would give the Commission powers to assess macro-structural weaknesses, deteriorating competitiveness and emerging macroeconomic imbalances; in particularly serious cases, the Commission would recommend placing the member state in an 'excessive imbalances position'. This would then trigger the 'corrective arm', whereby the respective member state would be subject to stricter surveillance, with policy recommendations then issued by the Council and the requirement to report to the ECOFIN and Eurogroup on progress in implementing the necessary reforms.

The Commission also proposed to establish a European Semester: 'Under the European Semester, complementarity of national economic policy plans [would be] ensured at the European level through policy guidance before final decisions on the budget for the following year are taken in member states' (Commission, 2010e, p.11). This would enable a 'horizontal' assessment of national fiscal policy, with special attention to the aggregate stance in cases of serious economic stress in the Euro area. As the Task Force subsequently concluded, this was the 'biggest reform of the Economic and Monetary Union since the Euro was created' (van Rompuy, 2010).

Equally significant though, particularly in relation to the argument of this book, was the Council's decision (28–29 October) on how the enforcement mechanisms would be activated: this would now involve 'reversed majority rule', whereby a Commission recommendation on sanctions would proceed *unless* a qualified majority of member states in the Council voted against it. For those unfamiliar with the idiosyncrasies of EU policymaking, this had two potential implications: the first, and most likely, was that sanctions would proceed unless the larger 'core' countries (such as France and Germany) vetoed them, meaning a loss of powers for smaller countries; but it also, secondly, increased the powers of initiation of the Commission itself. The significance of this move should not be underestimated. Chancellor Merkel had long favoured the strengthening of the EU's *economic* pillar, but had resisted the imposition of more *automatic* measures. On 18 October then, President Sarkozy and Merkel issued a joint statement in support of the increased sanctions of the preventive and corrective arms, but indicated that this should be enacted through Qualified Majority Voting in the Council (Franco-German Declaration, 2010; *Irish Times*, 2010). Indeed, Christine Lagarde (then French Finance Minister) argued that the automaticity of the rules was an altogether bad idea, saying 'To foresee a complete automaticity, a power totally in the hands of the experts, no. We believe that the political power, the political appreciation should remain fully in the game' (Euractiv, 2010). Quasi-automatic sanctions were however a key component of the Commission's earlier proposals, with the aim of reducing political discretion, in a move

DOI: 10.1057/9781137298010

which the ECB also favoured.[6] In essence, the Council's decision on *reverse* qualified majority voting was therefore a compromise between the two positions. It reinforced the position of the Franco-German axis (and a limited degree of political discretion more generally) in the emerging economic governance architecture, whilst also constituting an incremental depoliticised shift in the powers vested in EU bodies.

The October European Council meeting had one final significance: agreeing to the European Stabilisation Mechanism (ESM), the permanent crisis resolution mechanism to replace the *ad hoc* EFSM and EFSF. Its aim was to safeguard financial stability in the Euro area, including a stronger focus on debt sustainability and more effective enforcement measures, whilst focusing primarily on prevention. We will return to this in greater detail in the following chapter.

As 2011 unfolded, state managers continued to pursue two interwoven strategies: resorting to an increasingly high-level, opaque policymaking; and invoking the crisis as an exogenous imperative. The result was the monopolisation of key decisions by the European Council (Schmidt, 2012), such that the executive federalism of the Lisbon treaty had given way to an outright intergovernmental rule by the European Council (Habermas, 2011b). As Slavoj Zizek (2010, pp.86–87) put it, Europe appeared to be entering 'a period in which a kind of economic state of emergency [was] becoming permanent: turning into a constant, a way of life ... [bringing] with it the threat of far more savage austerity measures, cuts in benefits, diminishing health and education services and more precarious employment'.

The first cycle of coordination of the macroeconomic, budgetary and structural reform policies under the European Semester reflected this. It began with the Commission examining national reform strategies and publishing its Annual Growth Survey. Yet the order of the priorities was once more illuminating: with fiscal consolidation required to 'restore confidence by preventing a vicious cycle of unsustainable debt, disruption of financial markets and low economic growth' (Commission, 2010g, pp.4–8). The logic was clear: as President Barroso later explained to the European Parliament (23 March), 'Without fiscal consolidation, there is no confidence, without confidence there are no investments, without investments there is no growth' (Barroso, 2011a). The German-led consensus on debt reduction in response to financial speculation was in the driving seat.

Indeed, there was clear evidence as 2011 progressed that the severity and longevity – by which we mean the ongoing economic instability and

DOI: 10.1057/9781137298010

the growing civil unrest – was driving an ever-more radical agenda. This was especially apparent in the Franco-German 'Pact for Competitiveness'. At face value it was simply a new agreement on proposals to strengthen policy coordination and fiscal discipline. On closer inspection though, the paper required member states to abolish their wage indexation systems because certain members' 'competition deficits' represented 'a danger to the financial stability of the Eurozone' (Franco-German Declaration, 2011, p.1). Moreover, it also demanded that other members introduce constitutional reforms similar to the German 'golden rule' of balancing the budget. Predictably, the proposals provoked intense opposition. Not only did they constitute 'a radical reduction of the sovereignty of other EU countries', as indicated by Czech President Vaclav Klaus, but they were also the product of an entirely undemocratic process on the part of French and German elites (Klaus, 2011; European Left, 2011). France and Germany had effectively re-written European economic policy 'behind closed doors' (Euractiv, 2011).

Though the final 'Pact for the Euro' was a somewhat watered-down version (see Council, 2011a), it nonetheless formed a focal point for the groundswell of national protest movements. Yet even these more radical efforts left markets unconvinced, both of state managers' ability to construct a coherent, depoliticised strategy, and of their ability to contain the growing unrest. The twofold crises of coherence and legitimacy that form the focus of the following chapters were in the making here. This meant that the threat of financial speculation continued to hang like a sword of Damocles over peripheral economies. Fitch ratings agency stated for example – in relation to Greece – that 'while [its] economic and fiscal performance under the EU-IMF programme has in many respects exceeded expectations, its heavy public debt burden renders fiscal solvency highly vulnerable to adverse shocks' (Fitch Ratings, 2011). Greece thus found itself caught in the debt trap. GDP had contracted by 4.5 per cent in 2010, and the recession was not only the product of a sharp drop in investment, but also in private consumption – understandable given the dramatic rise in unemployment (14.2 per cent in 2010) – and the decline in purchasing power and exports resulting from the fall in competitiveness.

State managers therefore remained cornered, caught between responding to the exigencies of capital whilst unsure of how to manage the politicised social unrest. Continuing to apply pressure to its member states, staff teams from the Commission, the ECB, and the IMF

DOI: 10.1057/9781137298010

visited Ireland (5–15 April) to conduct their first quarterly review of the government's economic programme. The troika broadly approved the progress already made, though they emphasised that challenges remained. They noted that real GDP growth was expected to resume in 2011, although more slowly than previously forecast, with strong exports leading the way – as a result of improved competitiveness and an upturn in global trade.

Yet by 16–17 May it was now Portugal that was once more in need of financial aid. Again, the EU provided loans to the value of €52bn, on the basis of a three-year policy programme targeting the three areas that had now become routine: fiscal consolidation, competitiveness reforms addressing labour and product-market rigidities, and measures to ensure the stability of the financial sector (Eurogroup and ECOFIN, 2011). Release of further instalments was made conditional on positive reviews of the measures undertaken. In 2011, for example, this would involve measures such as reducing the number of services, compensation schemes, and government subsidies to private producers; reducing funding in education; achieving savings of €550 million in the health sector; cutting unemployment benefits by €150 million; freezing pensions with the aim of yielding €445 million; reducing personal income tax exemptions; and raising VAT to achieve an additional €410 million. Amongst the other requirements was a proposal to reduce the operating costs of ten of the largest state-owned enterprises which posed the 'largest potential fiscal risks to the state', as well as accelerating its privatisation programme. Finally, long-term unemployment benefits would be limited to a maximum of 18 months, and labour-market laws would be made more 'flexible'. In practice, the systematic targeting of those most vulnerable in society was a relatively clear and consistent theme: for example, individual dismissals from employment would become easier (clause 4.5i); overtime pay would be reduced (clause 4.6ii); and compensatory time-off in light of overtime hours worked would be eliminated (Troika, 2011).

More broadly though, it was the persistent unease of bond markets that was particularly formative to the crystallisation of the neoliberal project. Indeed, as spreads on Italian and Spanish bonds widened – showing that markets were unconvinced by the 'meagre' appeasement offered by political classes – Commission President Barroso captured the dilemma perfectly. In a letter to the heads of state and government he noted that though developments in sovereign bond markets 'are clearly

DOI: 10.1057/9781137298010

unwarranted on the basis of economic and budgetary fundamentals and the recent efforts of these Member States, they reflect a growing scepticism among investors'. Consequently, the real task ahead was not simply the (more tangible) structural reform process or that of reducing the debt burden, but of the (more intangible) need for 'markets ... to be convinced that we are taking the appropriate steps' (Barroso, 2011b). The crisis was therefore not simply a debt crisis, but one of leadership, since 'the undisciplined communication and the complexity and incompleteness of the 21 July package' had actually heightened market uncertainty (ibid.). State managers thus found themselves caught between the 'remorseless logic' of the markets – driving for stable conditions for renewed accumulation and a re-configuration of social relations in favour of capital – and the resistance of the demos (Osborne, 2011).

Beyond the fiscal compact

As 2011 drew to a close, the headline was grabbed by the Council agreeing to an economic governance 'six-pack' on the 4 October. The Commission had hoped that their speedy adoption would send a decisive message to investors, yet the lengthy negotiations only confirmed the opposite: that slow political decision-making reflected both institutional complexity and a still-hesitant commitment to the neoliberal solutions being proposed. As we shall see in Chapter 4, the rising domestic social unrest understandably added to state managers' hesitancy. The centrepiece of the new legislation however, was the ability of the EU to impose sanctions on governments that refused to correct excessive debts or budget deficits (*Financial Times*, 2011c). Hailed as a radical centralisation of economic decision-making, the Commission's power to fine member states would only be blocked by a majority of votes amongst Eurozone states (EUObserver, 2011). Not only was this again symptomatic of a more coercive and disciplinary approach, but it also again replaced national discretion with European rules. As one Socialist MEP commented, this was an 'austerity pact ... that [left] no margin of manoeuvre for EU states for intelligent spending and targeted investment' (Udo Bullmann, cited in ibid.). An open letter by civil society organizations noted, further, that 'the proposals will enable EU institutions to make decisions on member states' budgets, economic policy priorities as well as on labour and social rights with little democratic debate, or accountability' (Attac, 2011).

DOI: 10.1057/9781137298010

Given the clear opposition of leftist MEPs and organisations, the framing of the measures was crucial to securing their passage through EU institutions. By emphasising their 'necessity' to avoid the failure of the entire European project, leading policymakers exploited this to polarise perspectives. Speaking to the European Parliament just prior to their vote, for example, Commissioner Barroso emphasised that 'the sovereign debt crisis is, above all, a crisis of political confidence'. Thus to restore confidence, he contended, 'we need stability and growth. But also political will, political leadership' to 'propose to our citizens European renewal'. The alternative to further integration was thus 'fragmentation'; the choice was – in his view – stark and clear since it was not Europe that had failed to deliver, but certain national governments. Within this broader narrative he then spoke of the necessity of the 'six-pack': stronger enforcement mechanisms and the ability to discuss national budgetary decisions before they are made; 'this mix of discipline and integration holds the key to the future of the euro area. Only with more integration and discipline can we have a really credible euro area' (Barroso, 2011c). The point, he concluded, was that the 'the markets' had sent an unambiguous 'message' that it was fallacious to think of a 'single market and common currency' whilst maintaining 'national approaches to economic and budgetary policy', because 'narrow national interests' had undermined the 'European project' (ibid.).

Moreover, this so-called 'market message' was clearly winning out over the demands of the electorate (a point that frames the analysis of Chapter 4). Since the onset of the debt crisis, for example, Chancellor Merkel had waivered about the prospect of greater centralisation. Yet by September 2011 she was increasingly vocal about the fact that the German interest was the European interest, with 'more Europe' the answer. In line with our argument about the gradual erosion of opposition, and the crystal-lisation of political resolve, she indicated that 'treaty amendments can no longer be taboo in order to bind the EU closer together' (Der Spiegel, 2011a). The relatively swift passage of the new fiscal compact through Parliament (28 September), Council (4 October), and European Council (9 December) seemed to confirm this (Council, 2011b).

Summary

As Europe entered 2012 however, it was apparent that a third phase to the crisis (or crises) was unfolding. If 2010–2011 were characterised by the

DOI: 10.1057/9781137298010

shift towards depoliticisation, the strengthening of centralised, supranational institutions, and the intergovernmentalisation of an opaque policymaking in the European Council, 2012 brought issues of legitimacy to the fore. Segments of European society, increasingly aware of the demise of democratic politics and provoked by the reality of selective intervention, began to test the limits of depoliticisation as a legitimate governing strategy. As we shall see in the following chapter, this threatened to turn the democracy and debt crisis into a crisis of the state itself.

Notes

1   On methodological nationalism, see Gore (1996) and the concluding chapter of this book.

2   This involved increasing the effectiveness of the public administration, stepping up pension and healthcare reform, improving labour-market functioning and the effectiveness of the wage-bargaining system, enhancing product-market functioning and the business environment, and maintaining banking and financial sector stability.

3   I am grateful to Paul Cammack for highlighting this point.

4   It should also be noted that the Commission had made the case for deeper and broader economic coordination repeatedly, including at the 2009 Annual Statement on the Euro Area, and the 2008 Communication on EMU@10.

5   Emphasis added. This was, of course, disingenuous, given the US growth was debt-fuelled, consumption-based, and the source of the entire crisis itself.

6   Jean-Claude Trichet, for example, warned that current oversight of EU states' budgets is too lax, and called for a board of 'wise men and women' to watch over budget discipline.

DOI: 10.1057/9781137298010

4

From Depoliticisation to Resistance

Abstract: *This chapter addresses the third phase of the crisis, as resistance to austerity and the new authoritarian neoliberalism swelled. It examines the successes and failures of these resistance movements, arguing that efforts directed at more traditional democratic channels have proven ineffectual. The political classes have, instead, only sought to further institute constitutional and legal changes to protect policymaking from social conflict.*

Macartney, Huw. *The Debt Crisis and European Democratic Legitimacy*. Basingstoke: Palgrave Macmillan, 2013. DOI: 10.1057/9781137298010.

DOI: 10.1057/9781137298010

The previous chapter argued that as the crisis shifted from a banking crisis to a debt crisis, state managers focused increasingly on strengthening the supranational institutional mechanisms of economic adjustment. This was primarily motivated by the reasoning that financial markets – representative of the demands of capital – were concerned that public spending incurred during the crisis – first to rescue the banking system and then in counter-cyclical stimulus packages – would weaken rather than tighten discipline over labour and money. As Peter Burnham (2011, p.499) noted, the 'tightrope state managers have to walk in this situation is how to intervene in crucial areas to restore profitable accumulation (recapitalization, nationalization, quantitative easing) whilst simultaneously withstanding demands to intervene in other areas to the advantage of particular groups (manufacturing industry, low paid workers, the unemployed)'. The new institutions therefore had a depoliticised bias intended to insulate the imposition of market imperatives from democratic influence. As capital had feared however, the selective intervention of the state served to (re)politicise segments of European society. This chapter is devoted to examining this struggle as it unfolded.

I begin with a brief overview of the character and spread of the resistance movements. This second section examines the successes (or rather the lack thereof) of these movements, suggesting that they reflect a failure of traditional democratic channels of political engagement. The third and final section then argues that this breakdown of democracy has, perhaps predictably, had a twofold effect: on the one hand the very rise of resistance has polarised elite views, crystallising the coercive and undemocratic consensus; on the other hand the consensus itself has only further fuelled social conflict. The risk is that, since depoliticisation seems the only appropriate response to state managers and yet appears incapable of overcoming the nascent 'legitimacy crisis', a full-blown crisis of the state may yet ensue. Herein lie the limits of depoliticisation as a governing strategy.

Rise in protests

Though Greece was clearly the epicentre the sheer scale of the public protests that emerged across Europe was noteworthy. The early and spontaneous alarm of Septembers 2007 and 2008 had subsided somewhat. Now, however, as electorates began coming to terms with the grim realities

DOI: 10.1057/9781137298010

of austerity, they were reacting to three features of the new statecraft gripping Europe: the first was the level of political protection for banks, mirrored by the apparent waning of political momentum for banking reform; the second was more directly targeted at the austerity doctrine as it took shape; whilst the third emphasised the failure of democracy. As such these three forms of resistance came in overlapping waves.

Given the argument of this book the first wave can be dealt with most swiftly. The fact that the global financial crisis had initially manifested itself as a banking crisis understandably sparked public alarm. The images of queues of middle and low-income families hoping to withdraw their life savings from failing deposit-taking institutions was as much a symptom of the state of contemporary Western political economy as the images of Central Park filled with the homeless during the Great Depression, or the miners' strikes of the 1970s, were for their respective generations (Macartney, 2009, p.112). More profoundly, it was the rationalisation of bank bailouts as a matter of public interest, on the one hand, that also later fuelled moral outrage, on the other hand, as societal groups recognised the cruel irony of selective intervention and the fact that the costs of the bailouts would ultimately be borne by them. This fed into the European arms of the Occupy movement, rallying against 'the greed of politicians and banks' (Indignados, 2012). We will return to these more fully in the forthcoming sections of this chapter.

The second wave of the resistance movements focused on austerity. Already by March 2010 rallies and general strikes were taking place across the continent. In Spain protests against raising the retirement age gathered in Madrid, Barcelona, Valencia; in France industrial action at airports and oil plants over the proposed closure of refineries; in Italy at car production manufacturers; and in Portugal over planned wage freezes. These multifarious and geographically widespread protests thus led one commentator to suggest that this European 'winter of discontent' could be just 'the start of the greatest demonstration of public unrest seen on the continent since the revolutionary fervour of 1968' (O'Grady, 2010).

Indeed by September 2010, it seemed that the relatively individualised national protests might be giving way to a fledgling pan-European movement as the European Trade Union Confederation (ETUC) organised a coordinated European Day of Action. The demonstrations in Brussels and other capital cities, under the slogan 'No to Austerity: priority for jobs and growth', were an attempt to 'send a message to leaders as they contemplated new cuts in wages, pensions and employment benefits to balance their budgets' (*Time*, 2010). ETUC (2010) highlighted the following sets of demands, which were indicative of this second wave of protests: they expressed the desire for banks, not workers, to pay for the costs of the crisis; for a 'more social Europe with more solidarity for European citizens'; and for sustainable growth. Suffice it to note that the concerns were sufficiently widespread to bring hundreds of thousands to the streets across Europe, with an even greater number of public sector workers involved in mass general strikes.

Indeed, judging by the scale and geographic distribution of the protests, resistance only seemed to intensify. By November, 100,000 workers took to the streets in Ireland in one of the largest demonstrations in the country's history. In particular, the protests were targeted at what they considered to be the incomprehensibly severe budget cuts required by the €85bn rescue package (*The Guardian*, 2010e). Then in December similar scenes were witnessed in the Czech Republic – with its biggest strike in more than two decades, whilst other protestors formed a human chain around the Commission building in Brussels ahead of the Euro summit where minsters were meeting to agree the permanent emergency fund. The goal was to symbolise the belt-tightening that they feared would 'destroy wages and welfare systems' (*Der Spiegel*, 2010).

Whilst the media's attention shifted to the Arab Spring as 2011 began, the proposed Competitiveness and/or Euro Plus Pacts of March 2011 again triggered unrest. This time ETUC organised protests on 9 April in Budapest, where EU finance ministers would be meeting to discuss coordinated economic governance. But this was preceded by a more violent affair, as demonstrators and security forces clashed on the streets of Brussels in response to the 'unacceptable' level of 'pensions, social security and work flexibility…put on the table at the European level' (Myriam Delmee, Bond van Bedienden, Technici en Kaderleden (BBTK) union leader, cited in Reuters, 2011a). Another union leader claimed that 'the European Commission's annual examination of growth as well as the competitiveness pact launched by German Chancellor Angela Merkel and French President Nicolas Sarkozy [would] drag wages and social rights down to dangerous levels' (EUBusiness, 2011).

As such, the Euro Pact provided an ideal focal point for the unions. As European finance ministers met in Ljubljana, Slovenia on the 5 April, Europe's trade unions organised to demand increased pay, in opposition to the programme of sustained wage moderation. Meanwhile, as French unions rallied against wage restraint and pensions reform (19 April),

DOI: 10.1057/9781137298010

Bernard Thibault of the Confédération Générale du Travail (CGT) argued that the Euro Pact 'has made labour costs the mechanism for exiting the crisis'; emphasising that 'the systems of social protection are not the origin of the international financial crisis – it is totally illusory to think that increasing social vulnerability will facilitate recovery' (Thibault, cited in *Financial Times*, 2011). Then, on 9 and 11 June protestors in Spain clashed with police as new legislators took office; and again, on 19 June 2011, thousands of protestors – in almost a hundred events across the country – took to the streets to rally against the Euro Pact (Reuters, 2011a). Finally, following the European Trade Union Confederation's (ETUC) protest in Brussels (29 September 2010), the Confederation staged a large protest on 21 June 2011 in Luxembourg ahead of the ratification of the Euro Pact by European Council officials (23–24 June).

Indeed, an online call for 'European Revolution' brought tens of thousands of protestors to the streets from Paris to Madrid, London to Lisbon, and Berlin to Athens and suggested that resistance was gathering momentum (European Revolution, 2011). November 2011 therefore saw uprisings in Greece (again) and Italy (again) over new governments' decisions to press on with the cuts, and a similar strike in Portugal. As the new year began, attention turned to the Hungarian constitution as 100,000 people gathered on the streets against the new legislation – associated with the financial crisis – that would effectively institute a new elected dictatorship. The Spring then brought a whole raft of further demonstrations, related to new property taxes (Ireland), pension reform (Poland) and transport privatisation (Brussels). This second wave of resistance movements was thus almost unprecedented in spatio-temporal terms. The puzzle at the heart of this chapter, however, is that in spite of their scale and spread these movements have experienced very limited success. I show this in the following section before explaining, in the final section of this chapter, that this was a failure of democracy that reflected and exacerbated the third wave of protest movements just as it fuelled the resolve of state managers to insulate the policymaking process from these social conflicts.

Successes of the movements?

Spanish indignados

I begin with the *indignados* ('the indignant ones') who were the Spanish arm of the Occupy movement. As we shall see, they were perhaps the

DOI: 10.1057/9781137298010

most consistent and outspoken movement of 2011, which also chose non-traditional means to voice their grievances. As the crisis escalated in Spain, with unemployment reaching 4.9million (21.3 per cent) in March 2011, and a sweeping overhaul of the labour market, a raised retirement age, and extensive cuts to social spending the first protests took place in May 2011. Not linked to any specific organisation the movement began through social networking (internet) sites, making it the first of its kind in Europe (EESC, 2011). Consequently, the protestors did not target or support any particular political party or view, but expressed a rather more candid dissatisfaction with the current state of their country. Indeed, their calls for 'real democracy' also deliberately eschewed traditional trade unions and media commentators as avenues for political activism (*The Guardian*, 2011).

Perhaps the closest the movement came to *direct* success occurred on 9 July 2011. Upon being endorsed as the ruling Socialist party's candidate for prime minister in the March 2012 elections, Alfredo Pérez Rubalcaba proposed that Spain adopt Germany's voting model in what was labelled 'a direct sop to the movement that spontaneously occupied city squares in mid-May, claiming that the politicians "don't represent us"' (*The Economist*, 2011). The change would have brought about a form of proportional representation in an attempt to address the disconnect between the electorate and their deputies. Unfortunately for the Socialist party, however, it lost the 2012 general election with the worst results in PSOE's history.

This only compounded the sense that leading policymakers were increasingly immune to the kind of challenge posed by the *indignados*. By the first anniversary of the movement (May 2012) other successes were therefore hard to gauge. On the one hand, the Spanish media continued to contend that the movement had failed, by focusing only on 'discrediting political institutions' without 'identifying clearly the alternative' (*El Pais*, 2011). On the other hand, the movement – which had now spread from the Puerta del Sol, Madrid to the regions – was 'gaining experience in coordination and communication' (Likki, 2012, p. 2). This kind of decentralisation of the movement aided two objectives: to promote direct and participatory democracy in the local sphere, and to 'retake the public sphere' as 'the space in which citizens deliberate about their common affairs' (Sanchez, 2012). On the former, the results included time banks – non-monetary reciprocal service between the participants of the assembly; and the 'stop forced evictions' campaign that prevented

DOI: 10.1057/9781137298010

approximately 200 forced evictions in 2011. Whilst on the latter, the movement had arguably lost a grip on the political battle over austerity (Delclos and Viejo, 2012). Put differently, a tangible impact on the policymaking process was hard to discern, though the wider socio-cultural shift towards non-market-based relationships was perhaps illuminating. We will return to this theme in the concluding chapter.

Finnish collateral

In Finland, resistance to the passage of the Euro-area bailout packages took a more direct approach. Through the course of 2011 the populist anti-Euro True Finns party made dramatic gains in the April elections. Partly as a result of this, the new Finnish government and its finance minister, Social Democrat Jutta Urpilainen, spelled out a plan that made further aid to the European bailout funds conditional on receiving collateral from Greece in return. Importantly, at this stage the consent of the Finnish parliament was still necessary for the European package to work. This then prompted other countries, including Austria, the Netherlands, Estonia, Slovenia, and Slovakia, to forward similar demands (Reuters, 2011b). When it emerged, however, that the collateral would most likely be drawn against the bailout funds themselves – meaning other Eurozone states would effectively be underwriting the Finnish deal – the other member states promptly rejected the agreement. Finland though, remained intransigent. With the True Finns continuing to lead in the polls, the Finnish Prime Minister insisted that his country would pull out of the entire rescue package if their demands were not met (Reuters, 2011b). Finally, a deal was struck on Monday 3 October 2011. This appeared to signify a victory for domestic opposition to the Brussels Leviathan.

The specifics of the collateral deal told a different story. The terms of the complex collateral model would involve Athens lending its own banks sovereign bonds, which would then be swapped and sold, the revenue from which would be invested in Triple-A (that is, better quality) bonds, which would be the collateral Finland had demanded. In exchange though, Finland forfeited the right to pay its share of the bailout costs in five tranches, meaning it was liable for higher interest costs. This meant that the points scored with the domestic electorate – at having secured concessions from Brussels – would cost Finland financially in the long-term. That said, the bailouts would proceed and the collateral deal would

DOI: 10.1057/9781137298010

serve its social function: allowing state managers to appear responsive to the national electorate (Open Europe, 2011; Bloomberg, 2011).

Federal Constitutional Court

Perhaps the most insightful example though is that of the referrals to the German Federal Constitutional Court. Here a clear struggle emerged between crisis managers in parliament and government on one side, and citizens and opposed parliamentarians on the other. At stake were the new laws aimed at rescuing the Euro, and the Federal Constitutional Court was responsible for adjudicating between the competing claims, as state managers deferred to the 'autonomous' legal institution. The Court, as a unique defender of the democratic principles enshrined in the *Grundgesetz* (the Basic Law), was traditionally perceived as 'an important institution for the protection of minority interests' (Sontheimer, 1972, p.165). Moreover, its role in applying the rule of law was also intended to transcend partisan interests, giving it an air of independence and objectivity.

Midway through 2011 a series of constitutional complaints were lodged against the aid measures for Greece and against the Euro rescue package (FCC, 2011). The complaints were raised by five academics and a Bavarian lawmaker. They contended that the bailouts violated property rights and other protections in the German and European constitutions, as well as breaking the 'no-bailout' clause in the European Union's treaty, which essentially states that neither the EU nor member states should take on other governments' liabilities (Reuters, 2011d). The plaintiffs were not alone though, they were symptomatic of a growing German antipathy to the idea of successive bailouts to 'profligate' debtor countries. Though the initial lawsuits were subsequently rejected – on the grounds that the new mechanisms did not significantly impair the budgetary autonomy of future Bundestag's – they paved the way for later complaints.

Indeed, by July 2012, the whole of Germany's socialist Left party threatened to file a motion to prevent the ratification of both the ESM and Fiscal Pact (Deutsche Welle, 2012). For policymakers, the temporary mandate of the European Financial Stability Facility (EFSF) had been insufficient given the gravity of the ongoing financial speculation. Consequently, the (ostensibly exogenous) imperatives of financial market turbulence had led to a new and more comprehensive set of bailout financing instruments: 'crisis [had thus] forced the necessary coordination... [acting as] the midwife to ... new institutional arrangements' (Rehn, 2010b).

DOI: 10.1057/9781137298010

Following this, on the 29 June 2012 the German Bundestag adopted the draft bill for an Act for Financial Participation in the ESM. A total of 37,000 German plaintiffs (in a group entitled 'More Democracy') this time rallied in protest at the removal of safeguards of 'parliamentary freedom to decide in matters concerning the budget' which would thereby 'transfer essential duties and powers to the European Stability Mechanism in a way which is incompatible with ... the principle of democracy' (BVerfG, 2012, §149). In response, the Federal Government contended that the complaints were unfounded, emphasising that the 'overall budgetary responsibility of the Bundestag is safeguarded' since the 'democratic supervision of the work of the European Stability Mechanism is largely effected by way of rights of approval and participation [so that] the *fundamental decisions* of the European Stability Mechanism are subject to approval in the German Bundestag' (*emphasis added* ibid., § 182).

The decision of the Constitutional Court was illuminating. Faced with a threat to both the future of the Eurozone and, more immediately, the new Fiscal Compact and ESM strategies, the German Court requested that ratification of the ESM be delayed, allowing more time to scrutinise its details (*Der Spiegel*, 2012). German policymakers reluctantly deferred to the judgement of the Constitutional Court (Bundesregierung, 2012). The prima facie conclusion was that 'constitutional democracy [was] fighting back', wherein the 'need to manage the crisis ... had clashed head on with Germany's constitutional democratic settlement' (Persson, 2012). The Court's decision (12 September 2012) was, however, ultimately providential: rubber-stamping the new Europeanised mechanisms with a *legal* legitimacy, it reinforced conceptions of economic necessity, given threats to the very stability of the Union itself (BVerfG, 2012).

The Court emphasised the importance of obtaining and maintaining Bundestag responsibility for budgetary decisions, highlighting that the ESM did not fundamentally alter the European Treaties that gave the Bundestag this role (§ 191–201). It then stated, however, that no absolute upper limit on German payment obligations could be derived directly from the principle of democracy (§ 200). This meant that it agreed to German exposure up to a limit of €190bn, as negotiated under the ESM and on which the Bundestag had – in principle – been asked to vote. Thus the Court focused primarily on reinforcing that any *additional* increases in German liabilities would require Bundestag approval (§ 206–244).

The technocratic interpretation of – in a narrow sense – the terms of the bailout were symptomatic though of a more far-reaching process reducing

DOI: 10.1057/9781137298010

the democratic and the political to a legal–technical judgement. The point was that this inadvertent example of depoliticisation diverted attention away from the Merkel government as architects of the Europeanised adjustment mechanisms. Yet it also revealed that the neoliberal mindworld outlined in our opening chapters, grounded in 'real' material concerns for the future of capitalist accumulation, was increasingly immanent amongst both democratically elected and technocratic officials across Europe.

Insulated from democracy

Beyond the immediate 'failure' of these movements then, their very rise only served to intensify the resolve of state managers as they sought to implement 'constitutional and legal changes ... to protect [the policymaking apparatus] from social conflict' (Bruff, 2013, *forthcoming*). This section now explores this argument. Effectively, mechanisms and legal provisions established early in the crisis continued to struggle to buttress market confidence, in part because capital remained unconvinced of the capacity of state managers to decisively overcome domestic opposition. This was because the rise in civil protests helped to 'change the intellectual climate sufficiently to make moves towards further market liberalization even more challenging' (Charles Grant, director of Centre for European Reform, cited in Reuters, 2010a). Markets were concerned that 'the propensity for civil unrest [would] act as a check on their governments' (Alastair Newton, Nomura political analyst, cited in Reuters, 2010b). The fear of popular rejection, should such policies be subjected to a democratic, transparent process, therefore made opacity and closed-doors the only option (Schmidt, 2012). Later policies thus reflected the new determination of leading policymakers to 'use the *full range of means* available to ensure the stability of the Euro area' (van Rompuy, 2010, *emphasis added*). As the debt crisis thickened and the coercive pressures of market discipline were enforced by state actors, social conflict surfaced and the crystallisation of a deliberately anti-democratic statecraft was the corollary. This was a spiralling yet antagonistic and contradiction-laden process.

Greek referendum

Arguably the most explicit example of this kind of policy-learning by leading policymakers was witnessed in the national referendum

DOI: 10.1057/9781137298010

proposed by (then) Greek Prime Minister George Papandreou late in 2011. The perils of distortive democratic demands in this case once more served to polarise the debate amongst state managers. On Monday 31 October 2011, Papandreou announced that he would hold a national vote on whether Greece should remain within the Euro. The decision would obviously determine whether the Greek electorate were – by implication – willing to stomach the next round of austerity measures linked through conditionality to the troika bailout. Yet Greece's ruling classes understood the dilemma confronting them: a 'no' vote would undermine the economic, political, and diplomatic strategy of the past three decades; without a vote Greece appeared, however, to be becoming increasingly ungovernable (Lapavistas, 2011).

The suggested referendum came as a response to the *Aganaktismenoi* (the 'Outraged'), who since the summer of 2011 had organised mass gatherings across Greece's major urban centres, dismissing the political system and demanding 'real democracy'. The extent of the protests and societal breakdown over the coming months appeared to leave Papandreou with little option. He needed 'immediate legitimacy for his actions' and by framing the issue in terms of economic imperatives – leaving the Euro area would likely herald social, political and economic ruin, whilst remaining within it would entail further cuts – the Prime Minister proposed delegating responsibility back to the people (*Der Spiegel*, 2011b). In so doing he would delegitimise the resistance if the people voted to remain within the Euro area. Indeed, Greek polls reflected the electorate's awareness of this dilemma: on the one hand 60 per cent of the population were against the terms of the bailouts; whilst, on the other hand, 70 per cent were against leaving the monetary union (*The Guardian*, 2011). In a certain sense, Papandreou's decision was therefore a clever piece of politicking.

What ensued, however, was quite remarkable. The immediate reaction, shortly after the announcement, was that markets plummeted, panicked by the prospect of a Greek exit (Reuters, 2011e). The following day (Tuesday), several PASOK members – the Prime Minister's socialist party – promptly resigned in disapproval, leaving Papandreou with a slim parliamentary majority. Then, on Wednesday, leading European policymakers – lead by President Sarkozy and Chancellor Merkel – issued an ultimatum warning to Papandreou that Greece would be refused further aid until it met its existing commitments (Bloomberg, 2011). Indeed, the ultimatum was also backed by leaders at the G20 summit in Cannes.

DOI: 10.1057/9781137298010

French Prime Minister, Francois Fillon, captured state managers' determination to restore market confidence by emphasising that 'Europe cannot be kept waiting for weeks for the outcome of the referendum. The Greeks must say, rapidly and unambiguously, whether or not they will choose to remain in the Eurozone' (cited in *The Telegraph*, 2011). The result was that, on the 3 November, the PM decided to abandon the referendum idea and promptly resigned on the 9 November (*New York Times*, 2011a).

In turn a so-called 'unity government' was formed, lead by former European Central Bank vice president, Lucas Papademos, who had also been head of the Greek central bank (1994–2002) at the time when the Euro was introduced (*Der Spiegel*, 2011c). As with Mario Monti (see below), Papademos was the preferred technocrat for leading European policymakers because of his avowedly pro-European leaning. His leadership was part of a more encompassing attempt to re-assure business and financial elites, and confirm Greece's commitment to the single currency, papering over partisan tensions in the process. His goal? To keep Greece within the Eurozone: 'I am convinced' he emphasised, 'that Greece's continued participation in the Eurozone is a guarantee for the country's stability and future prosperity' (Papademos cited in *New York Times*, 2011b).

From the proposed referendum, to the European ultimatum, and the appointment of Papademos, a clear message about democratic participation materialised. It showed that, even in view of the fact that a referendum vote would likely shift the burden of responsibility for austerity from state managers to the electorate, thereby providing a degree of legitimacy, both markets and leading policymakers were entirely averse to the prospect of greater democratic engagement. They would continue to pursue a strategy of less – rather than more – democratic participation; legitimacy would, instead, be established through coercion and a politics of 'turning a deaf ear'. I would therefore argue that this was characteristic of a qualitatively new wave of political responses, since it constituted a more deliberate and explicit attempt to insulate policymaking processes from democratic political control as a result of rising social conflict.

Italy and the Monti executive

A similar view of democratic engagement characterised the initial appointment of the Mario Monti executive in Italy.[1] Since the onset

DOI: 10.1057/9781137298010

of the financial crisis, one of the defining features of opposition chan-nelled through traditional democratic means has been the resulting fall of national executives. Initially this was, paradoxically, associated with the demise of centre-left Social Democratic parties. This was because 'modern European social democracy is so deeply imbricated with the system that is in crisis that it is in no position to offer an alternative to it' (Ryner, 2011). In Sweden, the centre-left experienced the worst electoral result since 1911. The right had gone from an unconvincing performance in 2002 to the twice-winning Alliance of the Centre-Right in 2006 and 2010. In Portugal too, following the collapse of the Socialist government in March 2011 – when it failed to pass its latest austerity package – the election of the Social Democrats (PSD) brought the promise of higher taxes and tough spending cuts to create 'a wave of confidence in the mar-kets' (Reuters, 2011b). Similarly the decline of the German SPD, which recorded its worst post-war election result in 2009, clearly revealed that social democracy was no longer an effective agent for political change of a more egalitarian type.

The case of Italy and the incoming Monti executive, however, is a par-ticularly illustrative example. It highlights the view that since the debt crisis is perceived to have derived from weak state actors, democratically elected officials are ill-equipped to provide the strong leadership apposite to renewed capitalist accumulation. Though only partially related to his leadership through the Euro-zone crisis, Italian Prime Minister Silvio Berlusconi was a casualty of this offensive. Initially, he had only narrowly survived a confidence vote, prompted by his €54bn fiscal consolidation plan and a rising number of dissidents within the PM's own People of Freedom (PdL) party (*The Economist*, 2011). Finally, on the 8 November 2011 the Premier failed to secure the necessary 316 majority on a budget vote, which lead to his resignation (Reuters, 2011c).

This was followed by a further (successful) vote (12 November) on debt-reduction policies in a move that was heralded by EU President van Rompuy as 'a major step in the right direction, containing the measures to put Italy back on track and, when implemented, to start regaining the necessary credibility' (van Rompuy, 2011). More significantly though, a new government led by Mario Monti was then formed. Importantly, the incoming Monti executive garnered a high degree of popularity with EU, ECB and IMF officials (Bloomberg, 2011). Moreover, the former Competition Commissioner set about warning domestic politicians that they would have to be forced to answer to the Italian public if they rejected the sweeping cuts that would end the debt crisis. Finally, it was also decided that a government of elected politicians was unfit for the severity of the task in hand. Monti therefore assembled a group of technocrats dominated by university academics, a bank CEO, and a naval officer; that is, ministers who were largely 'unknown to members of the Italian general public' (*The Guardian*, 2011c).

With this in mind, the perception that 'democratic scrutiny is a nuisance that should be avoided wherever possible' (Open Europe, 2012) framed the consistent bypassing of parliamentary processes that executives across Europe have pursued. In August 2012 the new Italian Prime Minister provided the most explicit exposé into this mindworld. In an interview with the German newspaper, *Der Spiegel*, Monti contended that 'if governments allow themselves to be completely bound by the decisions of their parliaments without maintaining some room for manoeuvre in international negotiations, then a break-up of Europe will be more likely than closer integration' (cited in *Der Spiegel*, 2012). He explained that although each government 'must orient itself' according to the decisions of parliament, governments also had 'the duty to *educate* parliament' (*emphasis added*). The imperatives of (international) crisis management negotiations meant that the stipulations of national parliaments were effectively only 'guidelines' that need not be adhered to in an 'entirely mechanical way' (ibid.). Though only partially related to a democratic challenge to the core executive, the appointment of the (interrum) Monti government clearly reflected the neoliberal strategy of depoliticisation, which defines economic policymaking as a technical process to be removed from democratic political control and entrusted instead to experts.

ESM

As alluded to in earlier chapters though, there is substantive evidence of this strengthening and depoliticisation of policymaking at the European level as well. Indeed, this book has argued that the supranationalisation of these mechanisms is itself a corollary of the struggles domestic-state managers have found themselves embroiled in. The example of the European Stabilization Mechanism (ESM) is discussed here. To recap, the ESM is the new incarnation of the original European Financial Stability Facility (EFSF), the taxpayer-funded central bailout mechanism (Council, 2012).

DOI: 10.1057/9781137298010

The EFSF was established by Euro-area countries on 9 May 2010. Its objective was to 'preserve financial stability of Europe's monetary union by providing temporary financial assistance to Euro area Member States' (EFSF, 2012). Importantly though, the temporary mandate of the Facility, confronted with the severity and longevity of the financial speculation in sovereign bond markets, compelled policymakers to push for a permanent mechanism. In the words of Commissioner Olli Rehn the 're-emergence of tensions in the sovereign debt market ... put the [temporary] financial backstops to [the] test'. The resulting permanent ESM therefore showed, in his view, that 'when really pressed by acute needs, Europe can act decisively and effectively'. Consequently, the ostensibly exogenous imperatives of financial market turbulence had led to a new and more comprehensive set of bailout financing instruments (Rehn, 2010b).

The decision to establish the ESM, however, to re-assure markets, showed at least three visible signs of reducing political discretion and democratic participation. Firstly, the management of the ESM was comprised of a Board of Governors, made up of member states' finance ministers, with little room for national or European level parliamentary participation or control (Allianz gegen den ESM, 2012). Secondly, the legality of the mechanism was highly questionable. The legal basis for the mechanism was article 122 of the EU Treaty, an article that was intended to provide assistance to EU states in the event of natural disasters or sudden energy blackouts (ECOFIN, 2010b, p.7; Open Europe, 2010, p.6). The ESM would function by widening the definition of emergency conditions, since ministers now argued that 'we are facing such exceptional circumstances [that] the mechanism will stay in place as long as needed to safeguard financial stability' (ECOFIN, 2010b, p.2). Moreover, contrary to the EU treaties that clearly specify that decisions concerning the EU budget should be taken by unanimity, this decision was taken by majority vote. In other words, no individual member state would have been able to veto this highly controversial package (see Open Europe, 2010, p.7).

Third and finally, the decision on which countries would qualify for loans under the ESM would be made by Qualified Majority Voting (QMV), meaning that no individual member state would hold veto powers. This was an important change from the earlier EFSF package. Indeed, the 'exceptional circumstances' appeared to have worsened, providing

DOI: 10.1057/9781137298010

the rationale for a further reduction in democratic decision-making. The treaty change clearly reflected this, stating that

> In order to ensure that the ESM is in a position to take the necessary decisions in all circumstances, *voting rules in the ESM will be changed to include an emergency procedure.* The mutual agreement rule will be replaced by a qualified majority of 85% in case the Commission and the ECB conclude that an urgent decision related to financial assistance is needed when the financial and economic sustainability of the Euro area is threatened. (*emphasis original*, European Council, 2011b, p.6)

As Chapter 3 indicated, in relation to the strengthened Stability and Growth Pact (SGP), the use of qualified (or reverse qualified) majority voting is part of a deliberate and strategic attempt to reduce the ability of dissenting member states to forestall measures that are deemed necessary to the very survival of a unified Europe. In the process, it is implicitly assumed that since integration is in the best economic interests of European citizens, leading policymakers can take any necessary action. The fact that the electorate oppose this is because they fail to recognise their own best interests (Muller-Armack, 1979, pp.146–147). Moreover, the fact that such decisions – to strengthen rules-based, depoliticised policymaking – are themselves passed swiftly and 'behind closed doors' is preferable to engaging in the complex and drawn-out process of securing their consent or acquiescence (Persson, 2012).

Summary

In short, the final section to this chapter has argued that this failure of democracy is, on the one hand, symptomatic of the growing concerns of state managers at the rising resistance whilst, on the other, further fuelling social conflict. The fact that these politicised resistance movements are failing to find forms of expression within the democratic apparatus of the state, coupled with the dual crises of coherence and of legitimacy confronting ruling classes, threatens to result in a crisis of the state itself. Herein lie the limitations of a more coercive and depoliticised statecraft. In the closing chapter I turn to the work of Rosa Luxemburg and Jürgen Habermas to discuss the implications of this failure of democracy for the resistance movements.

DOI: 10.1057/9781137298010

Note

1   Of course, by 2013 Monti had entered and lost the 'democratic' election. The establishment of the Monti executive in late 2011 however reflected a peak in market panic and public unrest.

DOI: 10.1057/9781137298010

Conclusion

Abstract: *This chapter returns to the work of Jürgen Habermas and Rosa Luxemburg to explain conceptually what we have seen exemplified in the earlier empirical chapters: that resistance through traditional democratic channels will experience only limited success, and that there are limits to depoliticisation as a governing strategy. Finally it turns to the writings on methodological nationalism to argue that a more substantive transnationalisation of resistance efforts may also prove fruitful.*

Macartney, Huw. *The Debt Crisis and European Democratic Legitimacy.* Basingstoke: Palgrave Macmillan, 2013. DOI: 10.1057/9781137298010.

This short book began with the puzzle that Europe appears to be gripped by two opposing movements, one pressing to strengthen the mechanisms of economic adjustment and the other resisting it. It then suggested that, in part, the separateness of these movements derived from two seemingly distinct sets of concerns associated with Europe and its debt crisis. On the one hand, *economic* solutions have focused on productivity imbalances, budget deficits, and bailouts. On the other hand, *political* concerns have addressed the growing democratic deficit and closed-door policymaking of European leaders. In particular, the book has sought to respond to those critics who argue that any *economic* solution will ultimately fail, without the requisite accompanying legitimacy in the eyes of European societal groups. The problem, as I see it, is that these critics have argued for a re-democraticisation of the European polity to fulfil the legitimacy gap. In contrast I contended that, from the perspective of European state managers, democracy is at the heart of the problems that precipitated the debt crisis and thus it cannot also be part of the solution.

Through a critique of the ordo- and neoliberal intellectual traditions the book has argued that the so-called economic solutions are infused with a conception of democracy. The resulting governing strategy framed by this neoliberal mindworld has been depoliticisation. It has involved a more coercive and decisive attempt to insulate policymaking from democratic participation. Where the above critics have therefore conflated legitimacy with democratic participation and consent, this book has argued that legitimacy (of sorts) is being imposed by re-configuring the state and Europe into less democratic entities, and through constitutional and legal changes that insulate it from social conflict (Bruff, 2013). Put differently, coercion and repression have replaced consent.

In this final chapter I seek to explore conceptually what we have seen exemplified in the empirical record. Namely, that there appear to be limits to the efficacy of depoliticisation as a governing strategy. I do this by turning to the writings of Rosa Luxemburg and Jürgen Habermas. The purpose of this chapter is thus informed by the pragmatic aims of the book. As such, I will propose three big conclusions. Firstly, I will further explain why the resistance movements may need to go beyond traditional democratic means. This is because the tension between accumulation and democracy at the centre of this book runs to the heart of capitalist society and the institutions of government. Democratic demands channelled through democratic appeals will thus almost inevitably be subordinated to the disciplines of capital. Secondly, I will show how and why

DOI: 10.1057/9781137298010

depoliticisation also re-politicises society, and discuss briefly the limita-tions to this form of statecraft. My third concluding argument though, is that the other major challenge for resistance movements is to overcome the *methodological nationalism* that continues to frame perspectives on the crisis. This worldview presupposes the separation of Europe into discrete national territories, despite the tendency towards supranational coordination and integration outlined in this book. Concretely however, it limits the ability for European societal groups to perceive their shared interests. A more substantive *transnationalisation* of resistance move-ments may therefore also aid effectiveness.

Recognising the signs of the times

One of the big debates to have captured political science at large, and recent contributions more specifically, is the role crises play in promot-ing historical change. From a variety of perspectives and with obvious nuances, rationalist–institutionalist, constructivist, and Marxian-inspired accounts have postulated that crises – or at least the *economic moment* thereof – arise out of the pathologies immanent within a particular mode of socio-economic development. Certain of these accounts are also united by their claim that, put bluntly, these economic patholo-gies only provide the pre-conditions apposite to a moment of decisive political intervention (Gramsci, 1971, p.184). As such, Colin Hay (2011) has suggested that this is the nature of the situation we are currently confronting in the UK. My proposition in this closing chapter is that this is also how we should understand the current European conjuncture. To coin Antonio Gramsci's phrase, 'the crisis consists precisely in the fact that the old is dying but the new cannot be born' (1971, p.276).

The key arguments of this book have drawn upon an analysis of the (German) ordo- and (Anglo-Saxon) neoliberal intellectual traditions to explain both the historical trajectory of European economic and mon-etary integration and more contemporary crisis responses. Chapters 2 and 3 traced the transition from renewed neoliberal structural reform during the first phase of the crisis, to the depoliticised statecraft that has characterised responses to the debt crisis (the second phase). Chapter 4 (the third phase) sought to question whether depoliticisation and a more coercive statecraft can secure the requisite legitimacy in the face of the increasingly politicised resistance of segments of European society. In

DOI: 10.1057/9781137298010

this closing chapter I explore the nature of the openings and impasses confronting state managers and resistance movements.

In the writings of Luxemburg and Habermas we find three important clues: the first is simply the sum of what we have already seen. Namely that at times of crisis the state abandons its democratic character in favour of its role as 'market police'. The class character of the state is revealed and the state takes on an ever-growing interventionism, despite the neoliberal rhetoric to the contrary. The second is that this paradox results from the fact that the democratic state exists in capitalist society, meaning that democratic interests will necessarily be subordinate to capitalist disciplines. The third clue, however, is that the class character of the state and its need to seek legitimation for its ever-expanding sphere of activity are at odds with a socio-cultural system that – with greater state intervention in previously 'taken for granted' areas – itself becomes gradually more politicised. The challenge of legitimation becomes progressively harder. I argue that these clues help to explain the limitations of coercive depoliticisation as a governing strategy, in part because it systematically erodes the very basis of its societal support. Moreover, the clues also help to explain why resistance channelled through democratic means will arguably prove less than effective.

Luxemburg: the contradictions of an expansive state intervention

The threat posed to state managers by the democratic power of the dependent masses was already evident to Rosa Luxemburg in 1898. Indeed, in her view democracy was essentially asymmetrically weighted in favour of capitalist interests because it drew upon capitalist society; that is, a 'society in which capitalist interests predominate' (Luxemburg, 1898[1973], p. 28). Yet it was the dynamics of this mechanism – internal to the state apparatus and its function – that are particularly important here. The paradox can be framed as follows. Essentially, 'capitalist development modifies the nature of the state, widening its sphere of action, constantly imposing on it new functions, making more and more necessary its intervention and control in society'. At the same time however, the state is, 'first of all, an organisation of the ruling class' (ibid., p. 25). The socially benevolent purposes engaged in by the state are therefore only 'in the measure that ... they coincide, in a general fashion, with the interests of the dominant class' (ibid.). But this 'harmony' also endures

DOI: 10.1057/9781137298010

only to a certain point of capitalist development (ibid., p. 26). Here we might think of social Europe and the decline of the Keynesian welfare state for example.

At the time of writing, Luxemburg had in mind the bourgeoisie's desire for protection against the imperatives of economic progress and competition. Yet she recognised that in the process of this struggle, the state takes a position alongside the dominant class. As she argues, 'it [the state] thus loses more and more of its character as a representative of the whole of society and is transformed, at the same rate, into a pure *class* state' (ibid., p. 27). This contradiction therefore runs to the very heart of the institutions of government. The result is that the form and means of its coercion move increasingly into a realm which is useful only to the bourgeoisie and, for society as a whole, have only a negative consequence. In her view, as soon as democracy begins to fulfill the role as *genuinely* 'an instrument of the real interests of the people' (ibid., p. 28), the bourgeoisie and its state representatives would sacrifice the democratic form in favour of a more coercive 'police state'.

The implication – and one that relates to the wider resistance movements studied here – was that any attempt to 'capture' the state apparatus through a reformist majority would only take account of the *formal* side of democracy, rather than its real *content*. One immediately recalls the fate of Social Democratic parties and the paradox that pre-crisis neoliberal reforms repeatedly emanated from purportedly centre-left executives. It also perhaps explains why *direct* attempts – like the Finnish collateral deal or the German bailout lawsuits – have failed, while implying that non-traditional forms of resistance – like the *indignados* – may yet prove fruitful in generating social change. This conclusion is also supported by the writings of Jürgen Habermas.

Habermas: the limits to legitimacy

Habermas understood, as Luxemburg had, that capitalist development (and crises) result in (and/or derive from) the growing realms of state intervention. For him, this had the potential to transform into a crisis of legitimacy for the 'basic bourgeois ideology of fair exchange' (Habermas, 1973, p.647). As with the ordo-liberals, he contended that state intervention derived from the dysfunctional weaknesses of the market mechanism that required more than simply political oversight but active enforcement. The dilemma was that, as with Luxemburg,

DOI: 10.1057/9781137298010

a wide participation by citizens in shaping the political will – that is, genuine democracy – would expose the contradiction between 'administratively socialized' accumulation and a 'still private form of acquiring the produced values' (ibid., p.648). To achieve the requisite legitimacy, therefore, a (democratic) system emerges that elicits mass loyalty but avoids participation. The result, for Habermas, is that just as 'economic' crises potentially emerge from the behaviours of capital and/or those of the dependent masses, the state also potentially faces a twofold 'politico-administrative' crisis: an *output crisis* develops if the administrative system fails to fulfil the steering imperative taken over from the economic system; whilst an *input crisis* develops if the legitimation system fails to maintain the necessary level of mass loyalty (ibid., p.655). Indeed, and this is the important addition, the functions accruing to the state apparatus also *increase* the need for legitimation.

Concerning the legitimation crisis, Habermas, with remarkable prescience, offered two further thoughts that are useful to our concluding comments. He contended that some of the legitimation problems encountered by the state can be avoided by appearing to make the 'administrative system independent of the formation of legitimating will' (ibid., p.657). This could be achieved through the symbolic use of inquiries and expert opinions, as well as resorting to emotional appeals – and here we think of the construction of economic imperatives surrounding the Eurozone debt crisis – or structuring debate to push uncomfortable themes, problems and arguments below the threshold of attention. The more coercive yet depoliticised policymaking processes that have emerged out of the crisis are just such an attempt, as we have argued, to prevent rising social conflict from permeating the state apparatus.

The follow-up point, of greater interest here, is that Habermas contended that there are systematic limits to 'attempts to make up for legitimation deficits by means of well aimed manipulation' (ibid., p.657). The state's encroachment into ever-greater areas of everyday life requires justification, yet this politicisation of the culturally 'taken for granted' also simultaneously opens these realms to political contestation by the dependent masses. Put differently, the ever-increasing reach of the state – necessary though it is to restoring capitalist accumulation – simultaneously exposes the state to criticism unless it can find further means to justify and rationalise its actions. Yet, and this is the punch line, such rationalisations can never be entirely ad hoc; they must, of necessity, be related and relatable to the socio-cultural system – the expectations, traditions

DOI: 10.1057/9781137298010

and understandings – of society at a given point in space and time. The relationship between evolving state policy and rationalisations and the socio-cultural system is thus inherently conflictual; it reaches crisis point, however, when the intervention and activity of the state is 'leaps and bounds' ahead of a socio-cultural system that changes more incrementally. As Habermas stated, a crisis of legitimation arises from the fact that the socio-cultural system is incapable of being 'randomly functionalized for the needs of the [state]' (ibid., p.660).

The contemporary significance is as follows. In short, depoliticisation, particularly as an attempt to contain social protest, is struggling to resolve the crisis of legitimation confronting the Western liberal-democratic state. Domestic state managers – and their supranational partners in the EU institutions – are engaged in a qualitative and quantitative departure from even the *formal* institutions of mass democracy that characterised the pre-crisis period. Moreover, state managers have decisively rejected many of the *substantive* means of incorporating and responding to the democratic will. Legal and constitutional changes have been enacted that partition-off loci of policymaking from those of social conflict and popular input. The challenge – and one that perhaps frames the key argument of this book – is that this risks creating a decisive rupture in state–society relations, since the socio-cultural system has not – in contrast – decisively rejected expectations derived from the post-war democratic settlement. The risk is that *if, as,* or *when* a critical mass of European societal groups refuse to accept the imposition of depoliticisation, a tipping point will have been reached, the result of which may be a full-blown crisis of the state.

Methodological nationalism

If what I have argued is correct and the course of action needing to be pursued by the state risks turning into a crisis of the state itself, I suggest that the outcome of *this* particular crisis is open-ended. Much will depend on the gestation of alternatives currently underway. Here I want to focus my final comments on a major barrier to resistance movements' efforts in re-thinking Europe: namely, *methodological nationalism* (see Gore, 1996).

To begin, let me explain how and why this worldview continues to permeate both elite responses and strategies of resistance. The key point is that the assumptions contained in this worldview inexorably dictate

DOI: 10.1057/9781137298010

their analytical and policy conclusions, thereby limiting perceived potential openings and effectiveness (Radice, 2000, p.12). In effect, the deep-rooted counterposition of national against international is both a result of the – simultaneously – integrating and fragmentary dynamics of capitalist accumulation. In its efforts to shrink space and time, capital also enforces a policy of divide-and-conquer, denying societal groups the ability to recognise their common experience. An alternative view, and one which is implicit in the analysis of this book, emphasises that the contemporary world economy, including the states that seek to regulate it, are first and foremost capitalist (ibid., p.13).

Though I am less concerned here with the effects of methodological nationalism on elite responses to the Eurozone crisis, it should be noted that here too there are profound tensions. On the one hand, state managers are pursuing greater *supranational* integration in the form of strengthened and coordinated mechanisms of economic adjustment. On the other hand though, the idea of structural reform in particular Euro-area economies already presupposes the separation of Europe into discrete national territories in a way that underplays the interdependency and contradictory unity of the relations between these national spaces. Indeed, state managers are keen to retain this national 'separateness' as a means to contain democratic aspirations.

This is because a more substantive *transnationalisation* of resistance movements would arguably pose a more serious threat to the ruling classes. At a most basic level then, European societal groups must reject the view that the most important differences are those between nation-states, which conflates the core with the advanced economies of France and Germany, and the periphery with the profligate free-riders of Greece, Portugal and Ireland. Instead we should recognise that capital, as the least territorially static force, requires and facilitates cores *within* the periphery, and peripheries *within* the core, as intrinsic to capitalist accumulation (Macartney and Shields 2011). The EU and Euro projects are thus only regional forms of organising what capital does on national, city, and household scales all the time: re-distributing upwards from poor to rich whilst segregating and fragmenting to compartmentalise resistance. The point is that methodological nationalism continues to blur the vision of resistance movements.

There is, perhaps, a glimmer of hope. Despite the strong forces fragmenting coordination and the realisation of a shared interest, the commonality of the real lived experiences of much of European society is

DOI: 10.1057/9781137298010

arguably the key. Here it is becoming increasingly apparent that austerity is touching the more politically active segments of European society and undermining previous legitimacy in their eyes; this is, if you like, the 'Squeezed Middle' (see Macartney, 2011). Put differently, notions of 'Social Europe' once held a certain plausibility, at least as a hegemonic idea, because the politically active segments of EU member states were relatively immune to the inequalities, and were net beneficiaries of integration, through lived experiences such as travel and credit. In this sense the disenfranchised and marginalised remained at the margins. Geographically, they could be found at the margins of metro-cities in the prison compounds of densely populated suburbs, as well as being located in the weaker and poorer peripheries of the EU. Yet the crisis is revealing to lower-middle and middle-income households the reality of the social–neoliberal compromise: that social sweeteners are subject to market discipline too. So when push came to shove, the benefits they derived from the good times are rapidly being withdrawn. In so doing though the neoliberal project is again systematically eroding the very social basis for its existence. In the process of undermining the myths of methodological nationalism I suggest that a more substantive and far-reaching transnationalisation of resistance movements may yet occur.

In conclusion, as Wainwright and Goulding (2012) opined, 'we live in a time when the economics of profit are facing a profound crisis of legitimacy, while retaining a deathly grip on the apparatus of the state'. Resistance efforts directed through traditional democratic means have therefore predictably struggled. Moreover, in response to the proposals highlighted in the opening chapters (see Schmidt, 2012; Simms, 2012), a new democratic compromise in the traditional form will also be unsatisfactory; social democracy attempted this and failed. The more 'positive' conclusion though is that, partly as a result of the lack of legitimacy, new social movements are also emerging with an explicitly non-market-based ethos. Further, the 'Squeezed Middle' of European society is also, I argue, beginning to transcend the limitations of methodological nationalism as a capitalist ideology. Yet these movements too will, at some stage, require political expression if they are to provide a genuine challenge to the dominance of neoliberal governance in Europe. As such, the current conjuncture still requires a moment of decisive political intervention. It appears as though state managers – effectively acting as functionaries of capital – are closing the door on democratic engagement. The question is whether and how an increasingly politicised European society will respond as a collective force?

DOI: 10.1057/9781137298010

Bibliography

Allianz gegen den ESM (2012) 'Das sind die fünf
hauptprobleme des ESM', Bund der Steuerzahler
Deutschland, Berlin.

J. Almunia (2009) 'Beyond the crisis: what strategies for
a sustainable economy?' Speech at Brussels Economic
Forum, *Beyond the Crisis: A Changing Economic
Landscape*, Brussels, 14 May 2009.

P. Anderson (1997) 'The Europe to come', in P. Gowan and
P. Anderson (eds) *The Question of Europe*, London: Verso.

S. Andersen and T. Burns (1996) 'The European Union
and the erosion of parliamentary democracy: a study of
post-parliamentary governance', in Svein S. Andersen
and Kjell A. Eliassen (eds) *The European Union: How
Democratic Is It?* London: Sage.

Attac Sverige (2011) 'No to the undemocratic six-pack
of prolonged austerity', open letter by 78 civil society
organizations, including France's CGT union,
UK-based Tax Justice Network, and Attac,
27 September 2011.

T. Barber (2010) 'Dinner on the edge of the abyss',
Financial Times, 10 October 2010.

J. Manuel Durão Barroso (2008) *Speech in Preparation for
European Council*, European Parliament, Brussels,
8 October 2008.

J. Manuel Durão Barroso (2010a) cited in 'The EU is an
antidote to democratic governments, argues President
Barroso', *The Telegraph*, 1 October 2010.

J. Manuel Durão Barroso (2010b) President of the
European Commission, Statement at the press

DOI: 10.1057/9781137298010

conference following the first day of the Spring European Council, Brussels, 25 March 2010.

J. Manuel Durão Barroso (2011a) Briefing pre-European Council meeting of 24–25 March 2011, European Parliament, Brussels, 23 March 2011.

J. Manuel Durão Barroso (2011b) Letter to heads of state and government, 3 August 2011.

J. Manuel Durão Barroso (2011c) State of the Union Address 2011, European Parliament Strasbourg, 28 September 2011.

J. Best (2005) *The Limits of Transparency: Ambiguity and the History of International Finance*, Ithaca: Cornell University Press.

A. Bieler (2006) *The Struggle for a Social Europe: Trade Unions and EMU in a Time of Global Restructuring*, Manchester: Manchester University Press.

Bloomberg (2010) 'Papandreou slammed by Greek Unions, opposition for requesting rescue funds', 23 April 2010.

Bloomberg (2011) 'Bund falls for third day as Papandreou scraps referendum plan in step back', 4 November 2011.

F. Böhm (1937) *Ordnung der Wirtschaft*, Berlin: Kohlhammer.

W. Bonefeld (1998) 'Politics of European monetary union: class, ideology and critique', *Economic and Political Weekly*, 33(35), PE55–PE69.

W. Bonefeld (2002) 'European integration: the market, the political and class', *Capital and Class*, 26: 117–142.

W. Bonefeld (2005) 'Europe, the market and the transformation of democracy', *Journal of Contemporary European Studies* 13(1): 93–106.

W. Bonefeld (2010) 'Free economy and the strong state', *Capital and Class*, 34(1): 15–24.

W. Bonefeld (2012) 'Adam Smith and ordoliberalism: on the political form of market liberty', *Review of International Studies*, 39(2): 1–18.

N. Brenner (1999) 'Globalisation as reterritorialisation: the re-scaling of urban governance in the European Union', *Urban Studies*, 36(3): 431–451.

N. Brenner and N. Theodore (2002) 'Cities and the geographies of "actually existing neoliberalism"', in Neil Brenner and Nik Theodore, *Spaces of Neoliberalism: Urban Restructuring in North America and Western Europe*, London: Blackwell.

S. Brittan (1976) 'The economic contradictions of democracy', in A. King (ed.), *Why is Britain Becoming Harder to Govern?* London: BBC.

I. Bruff (2010) 'Germany's agenda 2010 reforms: passive revolution at the crossroads', *Capital & Class*, 34(3): 409–428.

DOI: 10.1057/9781137298010

I. Bruff (2012) 'Authoritarian neoliberalism, the occupy movements, and IPE', *Journal of Critical Globalization Studies*, 5: 5–23.

I. Bruff (2013) 'The rise of authoritarian neoliberalism', *Rethinking Marxism (forthcoming)*.

Bundesregierung (2012) 'The way is free for the ESM and the Fiscal Pact', 12 September 2012, Berlin.

P. Burnham (2001) 'New labour and the politics of depoliticisation', *British Journal of Politics and International Relations*, 3(2): 127–149.

P. Burnham (2011) 'Towards a political theory of crisis: policy and resistance across Europe', *New Political Science*, 33(4): 493–507.

BVerfG (2012) Extracts from the decision of the Federal Constitutional Court of 12 September 2012.

P. Cammack (2007) 'Competitiveness, social justice, and the third way', *Papers in the Politics of Global Competitiveness*.

P. Cammack (2009) 'All power to global capital!' *Papers in the Politics of Global Competitiveness*, No. 10.

S. Clarke (1988) *Keynesianism, Monetarism and the Crisis of the State*, Edward Elgar: London

J. Coultrap (1999) 'From parliamentarism to pluralism: models of democracy and the European Union's "democratic deficit"', *Journal of Theoretical Politics*, 11(1): 107–135.

J. Daley (2011) 'This was the week that European democracy died', 29 October 2011.

Z. Darvas, J. Pisani-Ferry and A. Sapir (2011) 'A comprehensive approach to the Euro-area debt crisis', *Bruegel Policy Brief*.

C. De Gaulle (1971) *Memoirs of Hope: Renewal and Endeavour*, London: Simon and Schuster.

C. Delclos and R. Viejo (2012) 'The day after: the movement beyond the protest', 14 January 2012, http://roarmag.org/2012/01/delclos-viejo-indignados-2012-15-m-spain/.

Der Spiegel (2008) 'Europe sees three bank bailouts in two days', 29 September 2008, Berlin.

Der Spiegel (2010) 'Euro fears force Merkel to act', 29 April 2010, Berlin.

Der Spiegel (2011a) 'Merkel says EU must be bound closer together', 7 September 2011.

Der Spiegel (2011b) 'Papandreou is right to let the Greeks decide', 1 November 2011.

Der Spiegel (2011c) 'Papademos to lead Greek unity government', 10 November 2011.

DOI: 10.1057/9781137298010

Deutsche Bank Research, 'Towards a new structure for EU financial supervision', 22 August 2007.

Deutsche Welle (2010) 'Press review: Germany divided over Greek bailout', DW-World.de, 29 April 2010.

Deutsche Welle (2012) 'German government, opposition join forces to save euro', DW-World.de, 21 July 2012 .

K. Dyson and L. Quaglia (2010) *European Economic Governance and Policies. Volume II: Commentary on Key Policy Documents*, Oxford: Oxford University Press.

ECB (2007) *Annual Report*, Frankfurt, ECB.

ECB (2008a) *Annual Report*, Frankfurt, ECB.

ECB (2008b) *Financial Stability Review*, Frankfurt, ECB.

ECB (2009) *Annual Report*, Frankfurt, ECB.

ECB (2010a) *Annual Report*, Frankfurt, ECB.

ECB (2010b) *Monthly Bulletin*, Frankfurt, ECB.

ECB (2012) *Monthly Bulletin: Government Finance*, Frankfurt, ECB.

ECOFIN (2007) Council conclusions on enhancing the arrangements for financial stability in the EU, 2822nd Council Meeting, Luxembourg, 9 October 2007.

ECOFIN (2008) Council conclusions on a coordinated EU response to the economic slowdown, 2894th Economic and Financial Affairs, Luxembourg, 7 October 2008.

ECOFIN (2009a) Council conclusions, 2967th Meeting, Luxembourg, 20 October 2009.

ECOFIN (2009b) Council conclusions, 2972nd Meeting, Luxembourg, 10 November 2009.

ECOFIN (2010a) Council conclusions, 2994th Meeting, Brussels, 16 February 2010.

ECOFIN (2010b) Press release: extraordinary meeting, Council of the European Union, 9–10 May 2010.

EESC (2011) 'Los Indignados', European Economic and Social Committee blog, 26 May 2011.

EFSF (2012) European Financial Stability Facility, Brussels.

El Pais (2011) 'Indignados en la calle', 17 May 2011, http://elpais.com/diario/2011/05/17/opinion/1305583201_850215.html.

M. Emerson, D. Gros and A. Italianer (1992) *One Market, One Money*, Oxford: Oxford University Press.

ETUC (2010) 'Euro-demonstration: no to Austerity – priority for jobs and growth!' ETUC website.

DOI: 10.1057/9781137298010

EUBusiness (2011) 'Protesters clash with police ahead of EU summit', 24 March 2011.

EUObserver (2011) 'Parliament approves economic governance "six-pack"', 28 September 2011.

Euractiv (2010) 'EU closer to agreeing new sanctions for budget rule-breakers', 28 September 2010.

Euractiv (2011) 'EU chiefs trump Franco-German competitiveness pact', 28 February 2011.

Euro Area Heads of State and Government (2008) Declaration of a Concerted European Action Plan of the Euro Area Countries, 12 October 2008, Brussels.

Euro Area Heads of State and Government (2011) Conclusions, 11 March 2011, Brussels.

Eurogroup (2010a) Statement on the support to Greece by Euro area Member States, 11 April 2010, Brussels.

Eurogroup (2010b) Statement on the support to Greece, 2 May 2010, Brussels.

Eurogroup and ECOFIN (2011) Statement by the Eurogroup and ECOFIN Ministers on Portugal, 8 April 2011, Brussels.

European Commission (2005) Working together for growth and jobs: a new start for the Lisbon Strategy, Communication to the European Council, 2 February 2005, Brussels.

European Commission (2006a) *Time to Move Up A Gear*, Commission President Barroso presents Annual Progress Report on Growth and Jobs, 25 January 2006, Brussels.

European Commission (2006b) Implementing the renewed Lisbon Strategy for growth and jobs: a year of delivery, Communication to the European Council, 12 December 2006, Brussels.

European Commission (2008a) *EMU@10: Successes and Challenges after Ten Years of Economic and Monetary Union*, Brussels: Commission.

European Commission (2008b) *Communication from the Commission to the European Council: A European Economic Recovery Plan*, 26 November 2008, Brussels.

European Commission (2009a) *Public Finances in EMU – 2009, European Economy*, 5: 19, Brussels: Commission.

European Commission (2009b) *European Economic Forecast*, 10, Brussels: Commission.

European Commission (2009c) Quarterly report on the Euro area, 8(1).

DOI: 10.1057/9781137298010

European Commission (2009d) Commission assesses stability and convergence programmes of Bulgaria, the Czech Republic, Denmark, Germany, Estonia, Hungary, the Netherlands, Poland, Sweden, Finland and the United Kingdom, 18 February 2009.

European Commission (2009e) *Communication for the Spring European Council: Driving European Recovery*, Brussels.

European Commission (2009f) *Economic Crisis in Europe: Causes, Consequences and Responses*, European Economy, 7, Brussels.

European Commission (2009g) Communication from the Commission to the European Parliament and the Council: long-term sustainability of public finances for a recovering economy, 14 October 2009, Brussels.

European Commission (2010a) *Report on Greek Government Deficit and Debt Statistics*, Brussels: Commission.

European Commission (2010b) *Press Release: Commission Assesses Stability Programme of Greece*, 3 February 2010.

European Commission (2010c) Commission assesses Stability Programme of Greece; makes recommendations to correct the excessive budget deficit, improve competitiveness through structural reforms and provide reliable statistics, 3 February 2010, Brussels.

European Commission (2010d) *Reinforcing Economic Policy Coordination*, Communication from the European Commission to the European Parliament, the European Council, the Council, the European Central Bank, The Economic and Social Committee, and the Committee of the Regions, 12 May 2010.

European Commission (2010e) *Enhancing Economic Policy Coordination for Stability, Growth and Jobs – Tools for Stronger EU Economic Governance*, Communication from the European Commission to the European Parliament, the European Council, the Council, the European Central Bank, The Economic and Social Committee, and the Committee of the Regions, 30 June 2010.

European Commission (2010f) *Economic Forecast*, Autumn 2010.

European Commission (2010g) *Annual Growth Survey: Advancing the EU's Comprehensive Response to the Crisis*, Communication from the Commission to the European Parliament, the Council, the European Economic and Social Committee and the Committee of the Regions, 12 January 2010, Brussels.

European Community (2009) *Memorandum of Understanding between the European Community and the Republic of Latvia*, 28 January 2009.

DOI: 10.1057/9781137298010

European Council (2006) *Presidency Conclusions*, 23–24 March 2006, Brussels, Council of the European Union.

European Council (2010) European Council Conclusions, Brussels, 26 March 2010.

European Council (2011a) European Council, *Conclusions*, Brussels, 24–25 March 2011.

European Council (2011b) European Council, Statement by the Euro Area Heads of State or Government, Brussels, 9 December 2011.

European Council (2012) Treaty establishing the European Stability Mechanism, Brussels.

European Left (2011) Pact for the Euro: EL denounces authoritarian power abuse against European peoples, 25 March 2011.

European Revolution (2011) Online call by People's Assemblies Network, http://www.peoplesassemblies.org/category/european-revolution/

Eurostat (2010) News release: Euro indicators, 55/2010, 22 April 2010.

FCC (2011) 'Constitutional complaints lodged against aid measures for Greece and against the euro rescue package unsuccessful – no violation of the Bundestag's budget autonomy' Press release, Federal Constitutional Court, 7 September 2011.

Federal Ministry of Finance (2009) *Reforming the Constitutional Budget Rules in Germany*, Federal Ministry of Finance – Economic Department, http://www.kas.de/wf/doc/kas_21127-1522-4-30.pdf?101116013053

F. Fillon (2011) 'Europe tells Greece: "no money unless you cancel referendum"', cited in *The Telegraph*, 2 November 2011.

Financial Times (2007) 'EU plans market reforms to avert crisis', 8 October 2007.

Financial Times (2010a) 'Moody's downgrades Greek sovereign rating to A3', 22 April 2010.

Financial Times (2010b) 'Austerity pros and cons preoccupy markets', 28 June 2010.

Financial Times (2011a) 'Spain protesters turn anger against Brussels', 19 June 2011.

Financial Times (2011b) 'French union warns of discontent at "Euro pact"', 19 April 2011.

Financial Times (2011c) 'European parliament backs "six-pack" legislation', 28 September 2011.

Fitch Ratings (2011) 'Fitch cuts Greek debt to junk', cited in *The Irish Times*, 14 January 2011.

DOI: 10.1057/9781137298010

A. Follesdal and S. Hix (2006) 'Why there is a democratic deficit in the EU: a response to Majone and Moravcsik', *Journal of Common Market Studies*, 44(3): 533–562.

Forbes (2009) 'Spain sees risk of debt rating downgrade', 13 January 2009.

Franco-German Declaration (2010) Statement for the France-Germany-Russia Summit, 18 October 2010, Deauville.

Franco-German Declaration (2011) Pact for Competitiveness, unofficial translation DE-EN, 3 February 2011.

S. Gill (1995) 'The emerging world order and European change: the political economy of European Union', in R. Miliband and L. Panitch (eds), *Socialist Register 1992: The New World Order*, London: Merlin Press, Vol. 28, pp. 157–196.

C. Gore (1996) 'Methodological nationalism and the misunderstanding of East Asian industrialisation', *European Journal of Development Research*, 8(1): 77–122.

A. Gramsci (1971) *Selections from the Prison Notebooks of Antonio Gramsci*, translated and edited by Quintin Hoare and Geoffrey Nowell Smith, London: Lawrence and Wishart.

D. Gros and N. Thygesen (1992) *European Monetary Integration*, Longman: Harlow.

J. Habermas (1973) *Legitimation Crisis*, Cambridge: Polity.

J. Habermas (2011a) 'Democracy is at stake', *Le Monde*, 27 April 2011, Paris.

J. Habermas (2011b) 'Europe's post-democratic era', *The Guardian*, 10 November 2011.

P. Hall (2013) 'The Economics and Politics of the Euro Crisis', *German Politics (forthcoming)*.

C. Hay (2011) 'Pathology without crisis? The strange demise of the anglo-liberal growth model', *Government and Opposition*, 46(1): 1–31.

F. Hayek (1939) *Individualism and Economic Order*, London: Routledge and Kegan Paul.

IMF (2006) 'Article IV Consultation – Staff Reports', various countries, 2006, Washington DC, IMF.

IMF (2009a) 'Financial Stability Report', October 2009, Washington DC: IMF

IMF (2009b) 'Debt brake for Germany – could it be too strict?' Public Financial Management Blog, IMF website, 23 February 2009.

IMF (2009c) *Report on G7 Meeting*, 14 February 2009.

DOI: 10.1057/9781137298010

IMF (2009d) *A Mandate for Action*, address by Dominique Strauss-Kahn, Managing Director, International Monetary Fund At National Press Club, Washington DC, 16 April 2009.

IMF (2009e) *Communiqué of the International Monetary and Financial Committee of the Board of Governors of the International Monetary Fund*, Washington, 25 April 2009.

Indignados (2012) The 'Indignados' Occupy Together website. http://www.theindignados.org/

INSEE (2010) *Note de Conjoncture: au milieu du gué*, Paris.

Interview (2011) with BAFIN (German regulator), Frankfurt, April 2011.

Interview (2011) with European Commission officials (anonymous), Brussels, March–April 2011.

Irish Times (2009) *Spain Given Credit Rating Warning*, 1 January 2009.

Irish Times (2010) *Sarkozy Backs Merkel on Economic Reform*, 19 October 2010.

B. Jessop (2012) 'A cultural political economy of financial crisis: money forms, crisis displacement, and deficit hysteria', paper presented at the *Northern IPE Network*, University of Lancaster, 17 February 2012.

V. Klaus (2011) Czech President, cited in EU Observer, *Klaus warns Euro pact will lead to full political union*, 29 March 2011.

Kok Report (2004) *Facing the Challenge: The Lisbon Strategy for Growth and Employment*, report from the High Level Group chaired by Wim Kok, 2004, Luxembourg, Office for Official Publications of the European Communities

Lamfalussy Report (2001) Final Report of the Committee of Wise Men, Brussels.

K. Lannoo (2007) *Banking Supervision Returns to the Forefront: Crisis Puts Spotlight on Weaknesses*, European Capital Markets Institute, Brussels, 25 September 2007, p. 1.

C. Lapavistas (2011) 'Greece crisis: Papandreou's referendum is a gamble too far', cited in *The Guardian*, 1 November 2011.

T. Likki (2012) *15M Revisited: A Diverse Movement*, United for Change, Alternative Foundation Study.

R. Luxemburg (1898 [1973]) *Reform or Revolution*, Pathfinder Press: New York.

H. Macartney (2009) 'Disagreeing to agree: financial crisis management within the logic of no alternative', *Politics* 29(2): 111–120.

H. Macartney (2010) *Variegated Neoliberalism: EU Varieties of Capitalism and International Political Economy*, Routledge: London.

H. Macartney (2011) 'Crisis for the state or crisis of the state?' *The Political Quarterly*, 38(2): 193–203.

H. Macartney and S. Shields (2011) 'Finding space in critical IPE: a scalar-relational approach', *Journal of International Relations and Development*, 14(4): 375–383.

G. Majone (1998) 'Europe's "democratic deficit": the question of standards', *European Law Journal*, 4(1): 5–28.

G. Marks and L. Hooghe (2002) 'National political parties and European integration', *American Journal of Political Science*, 46(3): 585–594.

G. Menz (2005) 'Old bottles – new wine: the new dynamics of industrial relations', *German Politics*, 14(2): 196–207.

M. Monti (2012) 'A front line between north and south', cited in *Der Spiegel*, 6 August 2012.

B. Moss (2000) 'The European Community as Monetarist Construction', *Journal of European Area Studies*, 8(2): 247–265

A. Müller-Armack (1947) *Wirschaftslenkung und Marktwirtschaft*, Verlag für Wirtschaft und Sozialpolitik, Hamburg.

A. Müller-Armack (1979) 'Thirty years of social market economy', in J. Thesing (ed). *Economy and Development* (Mainz: Hase und Köhler).

W. Munchau (2009) 'Berlin weaves a deficit hair-shirt for us all', *Financial Times*, 21 June 2009.

New York Times (2011a) 'Greek leader calls off referendum on bailout plan', 3 November 2011.

New York Times (2011b) 'Economist Named to Lead Greek Unity Government', 10 November 2011.

OECD (2006) *Economic Policy Reforms: Going for Growth*, OECD: Paris.

OECD (2011) *National Statistics*, http://www.oecd-ilibrary.org/economics/data/oecd-national-accounts-statistics_na-data-en.

S. O'Grady (2010) 'Greece leads Europe's winter of discontent', *The Independent*, 24 February 2010.

Open Europe (2010) 'The rise of the EU's economic government: proposals on the table and what has already been achieved', June 2010.

Open Europe (2011) 'Collateral damage', OpenEurope blog, 19 August 2011.

G. Osborne (2011) 'Osborne urges eurozone to "get a grip"', cited in *Financial Times*, 20 July 2011.

T. Padoa-Schioppa (1994) *The Road to Monetary Union*, Oxford: Clarendon Press.

L. Papademos (2011) 'Economist named to lead Greek unity government', cited in *New York Times*, 10 November 2011.

DOI: 10.1057/9781137298010

G. Papandreou (2010a) 'Time to end opportunistic speculation', Speech to European Parliament Economic and Monetary Affairs Committee, 18 March 2010.

G. Papandreou (2010b) 'Time to end opportunistic speculation', European Parliament, 18 March 2010.

M. Persson (2012a) 'Democracy and transparency remain the biggest victims of the euro crisis', *The Telegraph*, 13 February 2012.

M. Persson (2012b) Personal Interview with Mats Persson, Director of Open Europe Research Centre.

K. Polanyi (1957) *The Great Transformation: The Political and Economic Origins of Our Time*, Beacon Press.

H. Radice (2000) 'Responses to globalization: a critique of progressive nationalism', *New Political Economy*, 5(1): 5–19.

H. Radice (2011) 'Cutting government deficits: economic science or class war?' *Capital & Class*, 35(1): 125–137.

T. Raunio (1999) 'Always one step behind? National legislatures and the European Union', *Government and Opposition*, 34(2): 180–202.

O. Rehn (2010a) European Commissioner for Economic and Monetary Policy, *Reinforcing Economic Governance in Europe*, European Policy Centre Brussels, 15 April 2010.

O. Rehn (2010b) 'What is needed from European Policy Makers Now? Building Europe's Economic Future' – EEGM Policy Dialogue Brussels, 1 December 2010.

K. Reif and H. Schmitt (1980) 'Nine second-order national elections. A conceptual framework for the analysis of European election results', *European Journal of Political Research*, 8: 3–44.

Reuters (2009) 'Greek/German bond yield spread rewidens', 14 December 2009.

Reuters (2010a) Charles Grant cited in 'Austerity protests may curb euro zone reform', 28 September 2010.

Reuters (2010b) Alasdair Newton cited in 'Europe faces rising austerity protests in 2011', 15 December 2010.

Reuters (2011a) 'Euro zone closer to new anti-crisis package', 2 February 2011.

Reuters (2011b) 'Tens of thousands march against Euro Pact in Spain', 19 June 2011.

Reuters (2011c) 'Berlusconi to resign after parliamentary setback', 8 November 2011.

Reuters (2011d) 'Germany's top court to rule on euro bailouts September 7', 23 August 2011.

DOI: 10.1057/9781137298010

Reuters (2011e) 'Greek PM ready to go, dump referendum, for Euro deal', 3 November 2011.

W. Röpke (1942) *International Economic Disintegration*, London: Hodge.

W. Röpke (2009) *The Social Crisis of Our Time*, New Brunswick: Transaction..

M. Ryner (2011) 'An obituary for the third way: the financial crisis and social democracy in Europe', *The Political Quarterly*, 81(4): 554–563.

R. Sally (1996) 'Ordoliberalism and the social market: classical political economy from Germany', *New Political Economy*, 1(2): 233–257.

M. Sanchez (2012) 'Losing strength? An alternative vision of Spain's indignados', RoarMag.org.

F. Scharpf (2010) 'The asymmetry of European integration, or why the EU cannot be a "social market economy"', *Socio-Economic Review*, 8: 211–250.

W. Schelkle (2010) 'Government responses to the economic crisis in the Euro area: a battle of the sexes between Marianne and Michel?' Paper presented at the University of Princeton, 13 October 2010.

V. Schmidt (2012) 'Democratizing the Eurozone', *Social Europe Journal*, 15 May 2012.

A. Sen (2012) 'The crisis of European democracy', *New York Times*, 22 May 2012.

S. Shields (2007) 'Too much shock, not enough therapy: transnational capital and the social implications of Poland's ongoing transition to a market', *Competition and Change*, 11(2): 155–178.

S. Shields (2012) *The International Political Economy of Transition*, Routledge: London.

B. Simms (2012) 'Towards a mighty union: how to create a democratic European superpower', *International Affairs*, 88(1): 49–62.

D. Snower (2012) 'A grand bargain to unify the eurozone', *Financial Times*, 15 October 2012.

K. Sontheimer (1972) *Government and Politics of West Germany*, London: Hutchinson University Library.

G. Soros (2012) ' "Germany Must Lead or Leave": George Soros' Plan to Save the Euro', *Der Spiegel*, 11 September 2012.

The Economist (2011a) 'Europe's most earnest protesters', 14 July 2011.

The Economist (2011b) 'Germany's debt brake: tie your hands please', 10 December 2011.

The Guardian (2008) 'European banks: Dexia the latest to be bailed out', 30 September 2008.

DOI: 10.1057/9781137298010

The Guardian (2010a) 'Greek strikes threaten plans to tackle debt crisis', 4 February 2010.

The Guardian (2010b) 'Euro rallies after ministers agree Greece bailout terms', 12 April 2010.

The Guardian (2010c) 'Greece activates €45bn EU/IMF loans', 23 April 2010.

The Guardian (2010d) 'Fury in Greece over IMF intervention', 16 April 2010.

The Guardian (2010e) Ireland bailout protest draws 100,000 to Dublin streets', 27 November 2010.

The Guardian (2011) 'Greek Referendum: Papandreou's gamble could pay off', 1 November 2011.

The Telegraph (2010) 'Greece's "worst fears" confirmed, says PM George Papandreou', 26 February 2010.

B. Thibault (2011) 'French union warns of discontent at "Euro pact"', cited in *Financial Times*, 19 April 2011.

Time (2010) 'Union Protests Put Pressure on E.U. Leaders', 29 September 2010.

Troika (2011) EU, ECB, IMF, Memorandum of Understanding on Specific Economic Policy Conditionality in Portugal, 17 May 2011, http://economico.sapo.pt/public/uploads/memorandotroika_04-05-2011.pdf

M. Upchurch, G. Taylor and A. Mathers (2009) *The Crisis of Social Democratic Trade Unionism in Western Europe:The Search for Alternatives*, Aldershot: Ashgate.

B. van Apeldoorn (2002) *Transnational Capitalism and the Struggle over European Integration*, London: Routledge.

H. van Rompuy (2010) *Statement at the World Economic Forum on Europe*, Brussels, 10 May 2010.

H. van Rompuy (2011) 'The economic and political challenges for Europe', Speech by President Herman Van Rompuy at the opening of the Academic Year 2011–2012, European University Institute.

H. Wainwright and R. Goulding (2012) 'Co-ops help bring economics back to the people', *The Guardian*, 7 November 2012.

B. Young (2011) 'The different historical trajectories of neoliberalism and laissez-faire liberalism', paper presented at the *European Association for Evolutionary Political Economy*, 13 March 2011.

B. Young (2012) 'Trouble in the Eurozone: whose crisis?' Fifth Annual RIPE debate, University of Warwick, 13 June 2008.

S. Zizek (2010) 'A permanent economic emergency', *New Left Review*, 64: 85–95.

DOI: 10.1057/9781137298010

Index

DOI: 10.1057/9781137298010

CPSIA information can be obtained at www.ICGtesting.com
Printed in the USA
LVOW13*2117151013

357112LV00005B/21/P